Crucible is published quarterly by Hymns Ancient & Modern Ltd.
Registered Charity No. 270060

This publication is in collaboration with the Church of England's
Division of Mission and Public Affairs; the William Temple Foundation.

Editorial board

Stephen Platten, Edward Cardale, Kate Pearson, Elaine Graham,
Malcolm Brown, Chris Swift, Carol Wardman,
Matt Bullimore, James Woodward, Peter Scott, Simon Cuff,
Jenny Leith (Reviews Editor) and Anna Lawrence (Managing Editor).

Correspondence and articles

Correspondence and articles for submission should be sent to Anna
Lawrence at Hymns Ancient and Modern, anna@hymnsam.co.uk.
Articles should be of about 3,000 words.

Subscriptions

(for four copies): individual rate £22; institutions £40;
individual international £40; institutional international £50;
Single copies cost £7.
All prices included postage and packing. Cheques should
be made payable to Crucible, and sent to: Crucible subscriptions,
Subscription Manager, 13a Hellesdon Park Road, Norwich NR6 5DR.

Tel: 01603 785 910   Fax: 01603 624483.
crucible@hymnsam.co.uk

Direct Debit forms available from the same address

ISSN 0011-2100
ISBN 978-0-334-03164-2

Editorial
Stephen Platten   03

Articles
Marriage in *Living in Love and Faith*   10
Robin Gill

A Lesbian *Living in Love and Faith*   20
Jennie Hogan

Now You See Us, Now You Don't: 30
A Trans Perspective on LLF
Rachel Mann

Divorce or New Birth?:   40
Living in Love and Faith and the Future of the Church
of England
Robert Song

Forum
Cathedrals and the 'Science' of Innovation: 49
Reflecting on a Coastal Micro-Initiative
Francis Davis

Book Reviews
Matt Bullimore, James Woodward,   58
Yin-An Chen, Simon Cuff, Carol Wardman,
Edward Cardale

Editorial

A Very Long Conversation...

STEPHEN PLATTEN

Bernard Levin was one of the most remarkable journalists of his day. He was intelligent, entertaining, perceptive and compassionate. Interestingly too, as a secular Jew, albeit with a continuing sense of spiritual quest, Levin showed a particular sympathy with Christianity and indeed the Church of England. Never perhaps was this more clearly manifested than in his *Times* article responding to the General Synod debate of 1987 focusing on Tony Higton's Private Member's Motion on human sexuaity. Levin's article concluded:

> 'I emerged with a wondering but intense admiration for this amazing body. The Church of England, facing for once a real problem, predictably and inevitably fudged it. But in the very act of fudging, it spoke with tongues. It will be denounced from within and without its ranks, for both cowardice and brutality; but the result was a victory for all the best qualities of this country. The Church is as puzzled, worried and uncertain as the rest of us; but in a strange way it gave us all a lead, if only that by telling us to be puzzled, worried and uncertain is the lot all thinking people, and it is no shame to confess as much. The Church of England - loving, muddled, holy, generous, wise, humble, well-meaning, daft, forgetful, brave, honest and absurd – is certainly not all right. But it is emphatically All Right.'[1]

Even this extract does not do justice to the power and richness of the complete article, which captures something of how Britain felt at that time. Of course, we now live in a very different world: that was thirty-five years ago. But what is easily forgotten is the protracted process through which, not only the Church, but the nation itself has been engaged in, in responding to changes in attitude to sexuality: indeed, the recent material from the Congregation of the Doctrine of the Faith

Editorial

at the heart of the Roman Catholic Church (spurning any blessing of Civil Partnerships), suggests that some still stand some way back along that process.

This extraordinary conversation goes back a very long way. It was Winston Churchill's Conservative government who, in 1954, set up the Wolfenden Commission which finally published its report during Harold Macmillan's administration in September 1957. Chaired by Sir John (later Lord) Wolfenden, a former Oxford don and Vice-Chancellor of the university of Reading, the commission's brief was to report and make recommendations on the two very different subjects of homosexual behaviour and prostitution. Vigo Demant, then Regius Professor of Moral and Pastoral Theology in the University of Oxford was a member of the commission. The report's recommendations were in favour of liberalising the legal framework in both areas. So, it recommended that 'homosexual behaviour between consenting adults in private should no longer be a criminal offence'. Much debate followed, including a famous exchange of views between Lord Devlin, a leading judge, and H L A Hart, Professor of Jurisprudence in the University of Oxford; their disagreement reached down to the crucial relationship between law and morality. In the light of these profound differences of opinion, the conversation continued to be protracted. Indeed, it was not until the Sexual Offences Act of 1967 (applying to England and Wales only), this time under Harold Wilson's Labour government, that 'homosexual acts', on the condition that they were consensual, in private and between two men who had attained the age of 21, would no longer be a criminal act. (Remarkably, 'homosexual acts' between women had never been declared illegal.)

In that same year, Norman Pittenger, a retired don, resident then at King's College, Cambridge, published his book titled *Time for Consent*,[2] which argued for a new and open attitude to homosexuality, from a Christian point of view. The first significant move in this direction came with the establishment of a commission under the chairmanship of John Yates, then Bishop of Gloucester; the commission's report published in 1979 was titled *Homosexual Relationship: A Contribution to Discussion*.[3] The Board for Social Responsibility was deeply divided in its response to the report which some saw as far too liberal and others as not liberal enough; the published report thus include some of the criticisms by board members.

Despite the less than enthusiastic response to the 'Gloucester Report', in the summer of 1986, the Standing Committee of the

Editorial

House of Bishops asked the Board for Social Responsibility to set up a working party to advise the House of Bishops on 'questions concerning homosexuality and lesbianism'. The working party was not to repeat the work of the Gloucester Report but instead to see where the Church of England was on this issue and to advise the bishops as they sought to bring healing and unity. Completed in 1989, under the chairmanship of The Revd June Osborne, then Team Vicar of the Old Ford group of parishes in east London, and a member of the General Synod. This report was suppressed by the House of Bishops and only became available for public consumption some twenty-three years later, when it was published in the *Church Times*.[4] The Higton Debate had taken place in 1987, two years before the completion of the Osborne Report.

The next key moment in the Church of England's marathon conversation came in 1991, with the publication of the report *Issues in Human Sexuality*. This came in response to the request by the 1988 Lambeth Conference that all bishops of the Anglican Communion undertake 'a deep and dispassionate study of the question of homosexuality.'[5] *Issues* was both a response to that request and a reflection on the pastoral situation then facing the Church of England. The report was accepting of same-sex relationships among the laity, assuming they were within a continuing relationship, but clergy, living with a partner, were effectively called to abstain from any sexual relationship.[6] In 2003, a subsequent discussion document was published.[7] This followed a polarised debate, provoked by Resolution 1.10 of the 1998 Lambeth Conference,[8] which, 'while rejecting homosexual practice as incompatible with Scripture.....called on all our people to minister pastorally and sensitively to all irrespective of sexual orientation.'

This most recent project follows the most unusual occurrence of the General Synod having 'refused to take note' of a report from the House of Bishops titled *Marriage and Same-Sex Relationships after the Shared Conversations*. (GS 2055)

This sketch of the terrain over the past sixty years indicates how difficult the debates have been both within secular society and within the Church of England. The landscape, however, has changed radically. The decriminalisation of homosexuality was the first step. Following that, attitudes and opinions within British society have shifted significantly, albeit on occasion slowly, within the past two generations. Civil partnerships were introduced, legally recognising

Editorial

same-sex and heterosexual partnerships alongside the existing relating to marriage. More recently still, the *Marriage (Same-Sex Couples) Act* of 2013 did as the Act's title suggests. Alongside this, the fact of gender re-alignment (often with the support of National Health Service treatment) and thus a broadening acceptance of this phenomenon has led to a further revolution in our understanding of human sexuality and gender norms. Terms including 'trans' and 'cis' in relation to sexuality would not have held currency in the 1960s and 1970s. British society has changed as have attitudes more generally.

Following the failure to 'take note' in the 2017 General Synod debate, a further response from the bishops to this complete set of issues was required. As Robert Song indicates in his response to *Living in Loving in Faith (LLF)*,[9] the project to which this edition of *Crucible* is responding is not a report in the same sense of the Gloucester Report or *Issues in Human Sexuality*, although it does share some resonances with the ill-fated Osborne Report of the late 1980s. Instead, *LLF* is a teaching document offering resources for the entire Church of England – 'all of us' as Rachel Mann describes it in her response. It is designed to engage with the issues such that, *at the very least*, we may disagree 'agreeably' and, with an intelligent background to the conversation. Resources include biblical studies, doctrinal reflection, some understanding of the 'tradition', societal attitudes and the scientific background. This may then lead, *at the very best*, to increased levels of agreement, acceptance and most crucially to a proper valuing of all, whatever our sexual orientation and gender might be.[10]

We cannot underestimate the cost of this process intellectually, theologically, emotionally and politically. In editing this issue, it has been clear that in such debates, power dynamics need to be acknowledged. There are long held positions and not living in accordance with them is still a matter of discipline. To enter the debate openly will make some more vulnerable than others. On a personal note, I reflect on this as the only bishop present in the House of Lords chamber, late in the afternoon of Thursday 27th February 2014 for a debate on *Certain Statutory Instruments* in relation to the Same -Sex Marriage Act which had recently received the Royal Assent. This was not an acrimonious debate – all the crucial work had passed through both houses. Nonetheless, the Church of England understandably came in for criticism and notable in relation to marriage in church. Note was made by the Baroness Barker of a particularly discordant note relating to the House of Bishops' Guidance on Same-Sex

Marriage. I had not intended to speak, but it was clear that silence would have been misunderstood. I noted that: 'For a Church that has a tradition that now goes back 450 years in what its has been saying about marriage, to move in a significantly different direction indicates a profound shift. There will be a variety of opinions, but that is an issue of great consequence."[11]

My point implicitly was that for a church whose doctrine is enshrined in its liturgy, her teaching on marriage has been declared every time the prologue to the marriage service is read. In less than two years, the Church of England was faced with an entirely changed situation.

On the broader issue of homosexual relations, relationships within the Anglican Communion have brought difficult unresolved challenges to unity.

These challenges relate to issues of cultural difference and cultural accommodation. In the 1988 Lambeth Conference a different challenge was presented by the practice of polygamy and particularly within some African provinces within the Communion. Ultimately, it was agreed that in the face of highly complex issues in certain countries and notably those with large Muslim populations, a hard line on this issue could have catastrophic implications both in terms of mission and of harmony within society. The conference voted for a position which allowed for cultural accommodation. Thus far, the Communion has been incapable of achieving a different sort of cultural accommodation on issues of sexuality. This remains an urgent and unresolved conversation. It is something to which Jennie Hogan alludes in her comment:

'If we enter this listening project spellbound by fear of the Anglican Communion's reactions there will never be any genuine liberation for LGBTQ+ people in the Church of England."

At the heart of Bernard Levin's piece from *The Times*, with which this editorial began was the realisation of a double dilemma. First was the issue of polarised starting points within the Church of England. How could a compassionate and just response be achieved? In the debate to which Levin was responding, Graham Leonard, then Bishop of London, spoke for the House of Bishops. Levin reflected that

Editorial

'.... it would take a powerful grip to wrest the debate (from Higton's hands); the Bishop of London was not a likely candidate for the attempt, but to everybody's astonishment, it was he who....doused Mr Higton's fire and cooled his brimstone.'

The second key point in Levin's article related to Church and Nation:

'....it (the Church) gave us all a lead, if only by telling us that to be puzzled, worried and uncertain is the lot of all thinking people, and it is no shame to confess as much.'

Fudge, in other words, was more subtly an indication of such uncertainties.

Yet again, the Church of England has returned to issues of sexuality in what has undoubtedly been a very long conversation. Augustine of Hippo, one of the Church's greatest teachers, seemed to be equally obsessed; it is after all one of the key elements which defines our humanity - maybe this time we are being offered a real opportunity through this very different project, once again, to demonstrate to wider society (which continues to have its own uncertainties) a proper acknowledgement of puzzlements and worries, and to seek a profound understanding which avoids trivial short-term responses.

Rachel Mann generously notes: '.....for the first time, I sense theological promise in what the Church of England ....is up to regarding human identity.'

Robin Gill also notes: 'The contributors have listened carefully to a wide range of experts and lay people, and the whole report (sic) is written with commendable tact and humility.'

Levin commented at one point: 'Yet as a record of a Church wrestling with its conscience, its teaching, its founders, its history and its place in Britain today, the debate could hardly be improved upon.'

Can we do similarly? Part of this process is continuous engagement. We would be very pleased to hear from you as the Church seeks to take this forward. Why not write to the editor so that we might publish further contributions to a conversation 'that could hardly be improved upon'?

Stephen Platten was the Bishop of Wakefield and chairs the Crucible Editorial Board

Notes

1. 'Synod and the Sinners', Bernard Levin. *The Times*. 12th November 1987. P.16.
2. W N Pittenger, *Time for Consent*. SCM Press, London.1967.
3. *Homosexual Relationships: A Contribution to Discussion*. Church Information Office, London.1979.
4. *Church Times*. London. January 20th2012.
5. Lambeth Conference. 1988. Resolution.64.
6. *Issues in Human Sexuality*. Church House Publishing, London. See paragraph 5.22.
7. *Some Issues in Human Sexuality; A Guide to the Debate*. Church House Publishing .2003.
8. Lambeth Conference.1998. Resolution. 1.10.
9. *Living and Loving in Faith*. Church House Publishing, London. 2020.
10. See particularly *LLF*. p.x.
11. House of Lords' Hansard. Thursday 27th February 2014.

Marriage in Living in Love and Faith

ROBIN GILL

Living in Love and Faith makes a very serious attempt to set out current physical and social science evidence about gender, sexuality and marriage, to explain fairly the opposing moral and theological positions espoused by different groups of Anglicans, alongside wider inter-faith and secular trends, and to avoid dogmatic conclusions. The contributors have listened carefully to a wide range of experts and lay people, and the whole report is written with commendable tact and humility.

The remit for this article is specifically to focus upon what this important and thoughtful report says (and does not say) about marriage – a topic that the contributors return to at several points.

It is evident from the outset that *Living in Love and Faith* considers marriage to be vitally important but, also, to be something that has changed over time and that is currently facing some significant social and ethical challenges. In various ways the contributors seek to establish abiding features of marriage, alongside a clear understanding of these changes and challenges. So they state early that:

> Family life has taken many shapes over human history and there are different forms of family life in our own culture and throughout the world where love and care are to be found and where people flourish. Nevertheless, the church sees in marriage the form of human life provided by God for children to receive the secure love, protection and nurture of their parents, and to learn to love. For the strength of the family 'lies in its capacity to teach us how to love', and that is one of its many gifts to society. Hence, the church promotes the virtues of sustained, committed loving through marriage (p.30).

And very soon they produce the following profile of marriage today in Britain from reliable sociological sources:

> More people are living alone. Fewer are marrying, and those who do marry tend to marry later in life. As a result, 'the proportions of men and women in recent years ever married by age 25 are the lowest on record over the last 100 years.' More people cohabit prior to, or instead of, marrying, to the extent that 'marriage without first living together is now as unusual as premarital cohabitation was in the 1970s'. Fewer children are being born to married couples. Divorce is beginning to become less common – not just in absolute terms, which you might expect given the smaller number of marriages, but proportionally: the lifetime risk of divorce for people who marry today is the lowest since 1969. The number of same-sex couples is growing, as is the proportion who have married. More children are being born and nurtured in families headed by couples of the same gender (p.65).

They note that, in this context of widespread cohabitation, together with increasingly secular wedding ceremonies, it is now less than one-in-five couples (most of whom have already cohabited) that marry in the Church of England. Nevertheless, they maintain that:

> For many in our society, marriage holds out an attractive promise of security, intimacy, and mutual care, legally protected and culturally valued. Data repeatedly show it to be the most positive context for the flourishing of children, although there is debate about how much of this is due to the parents being married and how much to other factors. It is not surprising to find groups who have in the past been excluded from marriage longing for its benefits, or simply longing to live in a society where they are not automatically excluded from a widely valued ideal (p.73).

They also claim that:

> When received well and cherished, nourished and nurtured, supported by others and sustained by God's other means of grace in the life of the church, the gift of marriage brings life with fulness and gives life with abundance (p.37).

Living in Love and Faith initially identifies three positive features of marriage to amplify this claim:

Marriage as a Gift

It is a gift given to bring life and to give life. God wants us to live fully and offers us ways to live that draw on God's life of love. The joining of a man and woman in marriage is a gift given together with the gift of humanity itself. It is a gift given 'at the beginning' – before God's people Israel were formed, before the law arrived and even before sin came. It is a gift given to all peoples. The Church of England has resisted practising marriage in a way that is inaccessible to those who are not baptized and active followers of Jesus Christ. Rather it has wanted to help everyone who enters into marriage to do so more truly and deeply – to receive more fully the gift that God has given (p.24).

Marriage as Mutuality

[Mutuality] reflected one of 'the causes for which Matrimony was ordained' set out in *The Book of Common Prayer* in its service of 'Solemnization of Matrimony': 'the mutual society, help, and comfort, that the one ought to have of the other'. 'Mutual society, help and comfort' run like a golden thread through the liturgies of the Church, ancient and modern, especially in the Western Church where the couple themselves are 'the ministers of the marriage' (p.26).

In this love of God, a man and woman have become bound to each other, each promising to seek not their own good, benefit or fulfilment but the very best for the other whether their resources are plenty or few, whether their health is strong or weak, when they are young with life ahead of them and when they are old with memories of their lives together. They make a solemn undertaking to serve another human being in faithful love throughout that person's life. Stability is the foundation of their mutuality (p.27).

Marriage as Fruitfulness

The creation of male and female and their union in 'one flesh' brings the capacity to conceive new life and to receive not only 'the gift of children' but also the responsibility for 'the care of children'. The intrinsic relationship between sexual union and procreation is one of 'the causes for which Matrimony was ordained' in the church's teaching and it is at least one of the reasons why the non-consummation of a marriage is regarded as grounds for its dissolution in law. The Prayer Book's liturgy includes a prayer that carefully weaves together the themes of marital mutuality and fruitfulness, asking that the couple may be both 'fruitful in procreation of children' and – so that they can provide the environment in which their children will flourish as God wills – faithful in 'godly love and honesty' (p.28).

Nevertheless, since the first of the Reformation liturgies, the marriage services of the Church of England have recognized that not every marriage will produce children. The 1549 rite notes that some women are 'past childbearing'. The Common Worship service allows for the omission of a reference to children being born, and not only for reasons of age. There are other ways than bearing children in which marriages 'share in the creative purpose of God'. Through the adoption of children, the love of husband and wife can embrace a child born of other parents and provide the nurture and care the child needs to flourish. A couple can create an environment of care for those in need and of hospitality to the lonely as they find 'such fulfilment of their affection that they ... reach out in love and concern for others'. Theirs is to be a love that overflows to 'neighbours in need' and embraces 'those in distress' (p.29).

For good measure they also suggest that what is often seen as the quaintest book in the Old Testament has something important to add:

> The Song of Solomon rejoices in love, desire and sexual expression without any obvious reference to procreation. Although we should not lose sight of the likely consequences of intercourse in conception, and all its implications for the family and community which the Song's ancient world would have known, the primary reference in its poetry of love is to sex as God's gift for the expression of the couple's love and the deepening of their life together (p.33).

There is much subtlety in this presentation of marriage. I suspect that many of us who are ordained identify with at least the first two of these aspects of Christian marriage in the addresses that we give at weddings, amplifying the words in the introduction to the service and drawing attention to the mutual vows that the couple are just about to make.

Yet are these, in fact, all abiding features of Christian teaching or even of Anglican teaching? The report recognises that the balance given to each has varied over time, but it nevertheless does seem to regard them as abiding features that go back to the New Testament and, in part, to the Old Testament. For example, this is the point that they make about the biblical sources for mutuality within marriage:

> We know there were some legal protections for married women, and mutual obligations for husbands and wives (see Deuteronomy 24–27; 1 Corinthians 7; Ephesians 5; Hebrews 13.4) (p.182).

In Deuteronomy there are, indeed, legal protections (including some, such as Deuteronomy 25.11-12, which now appear utterly abhorrent) and, in 1 Corinthians 7 and Ephesians 5, there are important features of mutuality (although not much of either in Hebrews 13.4). The report does recognise, in other places, that patriarchy has sometimes featured within Christian history. Elsewhere it also calls particular attention to Ephesians 5.25 and 5.32, but, surprisingly, it makes no mention anywhere of Ephesians 5.22-24:

Wives, be subject to your husbands as you are to the Lord. For the husband is the head of the wife just as Christ is the head of the church, the body of which he is the Saviour. Just as the church is subject to Christ, so also wives ought to be, in everything, to their husbands.

Similarly, it makes no mention anywhere of 1 Corinthians 14.32-36:

> As in all the churches of the saints, women should be silent in the churches. For they are not permitted to speak, but should be subordinate, as the law also says. If there is anything they desire to know, let them ask their husbands at home. For it is shameful for a woman to speak in church.

It would be difficult to think of two texts that have been quoted more often within Church of England debates in recent years – albeit within debates usually, not about marriage, but about the ordination of women. Specifically, in the context of marriage, however, these two texts suggest anything but mutuality between husband and wife and, among some conservative evangelicals, they are still used today to justify the subordination of women within marriage.

Perhaps the report is on safer ground when it later adds a fourth and fifth feature of marriage:

Marriage as a Rule of Fidelity
Married life can be thought of as a 'rule of life'. It, too, is a gift from God. It is one distinctive way of life amongst others. It demands of those who pursue it particular kinds of attentiveness, care and self- restraint. It is sealed by vows. It is, or should be, recognized and supported by the wider community. At the heart of this rule of life is the rule of fidelity: the commitment of each partner to be faithful to the other. This involves, of course, a refusal to have sex with other people, but it includes much more than that, too. It involves a promise of loyalty, and a promise of mutual care 'for better, for worse, for richer, for poorer, in sickness and in health' (p.244).

Marriage as sacramental
Marriage is very rarely referred to as a sacrament in the historic formularies of the Church of England... much Anglican teaching has therefore tended to regard it as *sacramental* – as having some of the characteristics of a sacrament. Sacramental actions don't simply point to, or tell us about, the mystery of salvation. They aren't simply parables. They are a means by which God invites us into that mystery and helps us to inhabit it – and so, in the Common Worship marriage service, marriages are described as 'a means of grace'. They are gifts from God, given to help us know more of God's redeeming and healing love in the fractured reality of our lives. The love that a couple experiences in marriage, and that they work at embodying and displaying, isn't simply something that resembles God's love. God is directly at work in it, drawing the couple into love and helping them to love better, and to love and be loved more fully (p.245).

Readers of this article will be fully aware that the main reason that *Living in Love and Faith* spends so long identifying these aspects of marriage is, not because the Church of England --or, more widely, the Anglican Communion -- needs yet another defence of heterosexual marriage, but because it currently has a major crisis about the propriety of same-sex marriage (whether the wedding ceremony takes place in church or not). On this issue the report deliberately avoids taking sides and is determined, instead, to put this issue into context rather than to resolve it. The contributors do this magnificently, but, in the process, they also offer clues that opponents and supporters of same-sex marriage, alike, need to ponder carefully. I would suggest the following:

Is marriage exclusively between a man and a woman?
The conviction that, it is, was the corner-stone of the House of Bishop's opposition to same-sex marriage legislation in 2014 in England and Wales and remains the corner-stone of their continuing prohibition of same-sex weddings in church and of clergy marrying same-sex partners. The report sets out the arguments of opposing sides well and studiously avoids taking sides. However, in one crucial respect, the contributors undermine the Bishops' defense of exclusively heterosexual marriages, by piling in scientific evidence about the fluidity of gender and sexuality. They, very properly, deny that science can settle such ethical/theological issues, but the very evidence itself does at least make it more complicated to define a 'man' and a 'woman' in polar terms. We all appear to be part of a spectrum and, if that is true, making some cut-off point between man and woman in the context of eligibility for marriage begins to look suspiciously arbitrary. Science here can, at least, raise suspicion, even if it cannot resolve the issue.

Can same-sex marriages exhibit the five aspects of Christian marriage?
The transcribed discussions of laypeople that punctuate *Living in Love and Faith* are particularly interesting here, especially since they typically include both straight and lesbian/gay discussants. Sometimes they conflict but, at other times, their views come closer together. Again, there is no attempt in the report to reach a resolution, but there is enough evidence provided to suggest that, once people with opposing views treat each other as people—and especially as fellow Christians -- then they can see more positive aspects of their different styles of living and bonding. Specifically, those Christians in a same-sex marriage do seem to report a very similar experience of their marriage as gift, as mutuality, as fidelity and as sacramental. Even fruitfulness (in the sense of having one's own biological children) has become a reality for same-sex couples, using the same inventive medical technologies that have helped many otherwise infertile heterosexual couples to have biological children.

Is it fair or even wise to exclude lesbian and gay Christians from marriage? Living in Love and Faith refrains from any direct criticism of the House of Bishop's 1991 report *Issues in Human Sexuality* -- a document (even when revised in 2004) that may have contributed unwittingly to the culture of secrecy within the Church of England that has left an appalling legacy of unreported clerical sexual abuse -- not least because, in effect, it encouraged some ordination candidates not to be frank about their sexuality and Bishops not to ask. Yet *Living in Love and Faith* does have this very telling paragraph:

> *Issues in Human Sexuality* claimed both that 'Homosexual people are in every way as valuable to and as valued by God as heterosexual people' and that 'Homophile orientation and its expression in sexual activity do not constitute a parallel and alternative form of human sexuality as complete within the terms of the created order as the heterosexual'. For some, there is an irreconcilable tension here: homosexual people are told that they are of equal dignity, and yet that there is something incomplete about them compared to heterosexual people, and that they are excluded from a whole realm of intimate relationships that are open to (and highly valued by) others. Many lesbians, gays, bisexuals and others have experienced this as a relegation to second-class status and as a denial that they can belong as fully as others to the body of Christ. Others agree with the report that both of these principles need to be upheld and that they cohere. Any person is as valuable to and as valued by God as any other, no matter what they desire or do, but some patterns of human desire – here sexual orientations – and some forms of human conduct – here patterns of sexual behaviour – are more in tune with God's purposes for human beings than others (p.196).

It also notes that gay and lesbian Christians maintain that:

> [Celibacy is] something that is being imposed by the church as if it were a gift or a freely chosen commitment. They recognize that celibacy can be for some a gift and calling from God, but they deny that this gift and calling are automatically given to lesbian and gay people. And some argue that to impose such a pathway on people while calling it a gift or celebrating it as a calling makes it harder for those affected to be honest about their experience

and about the cost and pain of what is demanded from them. They also sometimes find that their criticisms are treated as if they were rejecting the whole idea of self-denial, or the whole idea that discipleship demands discipline and transformation. The argument, however, is not about whether discipline and self-denial are called for from Jesus' disciples, nor whether celibacy is a discipline that is required in some circumstances and that, for some, might be a valued element of a particular vocation. The argument is about whether celibacy is the only appropriate expression of discipleship for lesbian and gay people – and these Christians answer that it is no more and no less of a possibility than it is for heterosexual people (p.241).

In the context of current safeguarding scandals, imposing sexual abstinence for life upon lesbian and gay clergy should surely be a matter of considerable concern. Indeed, those of us who have been blessed with long and happy marriages might well ponder why we would wish to deny such sacramental blessedness and human joy to gays and lesbians. Ever since Cranmer, Anglican ordained ministry has been emphatically uxorious (in his case secretively so) -- realizing that enforced clerical celibacy has ill served our Roman Catholic friends. And, after the enduring scandal of Bishop Peter Ball, it is obvious that even self-imposed vocational celibacy among Anglican clergy needs very careful safeguarding. The Ball twins' monastic order, much praised when they founded it, manifestly and woefully lacked that.

Of course, the contributors are well aware that a change of policy on same-sex marriage is fraught with danger for any Church. Yet they note that vexatious changes *have* been made by Anglican authorities in the past – for example, on contraception at the Lambeth Conference in 1930, on polygamy in Africa and, more recently (and slowly) on marriage after divorce. They leave the door ajar for a similar change on same-sex marriages in churches, realising, perhaps, that, as churchgoers in Britain become more and more accepting (not least because they have family members who are lesbian or gay), then a compassionate (but sadly flawed) Church may eventually need to change -- just as it did, despite serious misgivings by more conservative church members, on contraception, divorce and African polygamy.

This significant and welcome report ends with the following call to the Church of England:

To attend to the "'mind" of the church means reading the Bible together in the light of the creeds and the history of authoritative teachings from the Christian past… It means reading in the midst of worship, which directs our hearts and minds to the love of God and shapes our imagination of the whole Christian story. It means listening to one another – to the whole community of Christ's … including those often excluded from the conversations of the Church… The more we hear of his voice, the deeper we can be drawn into the abundant life of love and faith that God has for us (p.330).

Amen to that.

Robin Gill is Emeritus Professor of Applied Theology at the University of Kent, Editor of Theology *and Canon Theologian at Holy Trinity Cathedral Gibraltar.*

A Lesbian Living in Love and Faith

Jennie Hogan

Admittedly, I had a heavy heart when looking online at the LLF material for the first time. To be even more honest, I may not have dared to look at them were it not for writing this article. The website is slick and stylish; the short films are well made and engaging; the hefty book seeks to entertain with its large font and flashy images; the course booklet is fresh and mightily accessible. And still, a creeping dread arose each time I read, watched or listened to these carefully and ambitiously constructed resources.

I want to reflect on the LLF project from lesbian, feminist and queer perspectives. I will question the aims and expectations of this ambitious project and highlight some concerning absences. This paper will include personal reflections in response to LLF, not least because it is important to explore the potential personal and emotional impact LLF may have on certain people, most especially marginalised communities and individuals.

I have not spent much time talking about sexuality and gender amongst evangelical Christians; in fact, I steer clear. At deanery chapters amongst fellow clergy I am well aware of who amongst us has a clear view that homosexuality is a sin. We never talk about this and if I were invited to attend an LLF group with them I would most probably decline. Whether being LGBTQ+ is good or sinful is not an argument with which I want to engage, let alone win. The way I live as a lesbian Christian is not a topic to be debated. It is as absurd, for instance, as asking, 'Should people of different races be treated equally?' Or, 'Should left-handed people be able to go to school?' Whilst this may sound rather far-fetched, it is equally as bizarre to be asking whether or not it is possible for me to express and live out my desire whilst also attempting faithfully to walk the way of Jesus Christ.

I am aware that these introductory reflections may seem rather stark but I contend that these deep divisions are not easily mended by speaking openly and listening carefully. The question that keeps returning to me is: 'what does the Church honestly hope this project will achieve?' Over the years I have found the Church's wrangling over sexuality and homosexuality in particular, disturbing and offensive. It feels as though complete strangers, whom we are repeatedly told in LLF - make us brothers and sisters in Christ, can decide whether the way I live, dream, desire and feel, is *good* or not.

The pervasive reality of homophobia

A cogent summary in the LLF book surveys the historic debates that have taken place in Church Synod about gender and sexuality, and they make for grim reading. Seventeen years after ordination I now recognize that had I exposed myself to these reports in great detail I may not have said 'I do' at St Paul's Cathedral at my ordination. There is no doubt that the Church's rules sometimes do not match reality, which in some ways offers me more than a modicum of comfort. Everyone knows that without LGBTQ+ clergy the Church would collapse, or at least be deeply impoverished. This needs to be admitted otherwise the charge of gross hypocrisy is irrefutable.

The Bishops open the LLF book with 'An invitation'. They look to the feeding of the 5000 when Jesus instructs his disciples to 'Make the people sit down' (John 6.10) as an encouragement for everyone to engage in this project no matter how uncomfortable this may feel. But my question, 'to what end?' keeps recurring. The Archbishops of Canterbury and York, who have jointly written the book's Foreword, offer encouragement to 'Be of the same mind.' (Phil. 2: 4-13) but it feels like a controlling, though by no means dishonest desire for agreement in spite of the suffering this may cause. However, they offer some important context: The report 'Marriage and Same -Sex relationships' was declined by the General Synod in 2017. The Bishops reacted to this unusual situation publishing a joint letter which includes the following plea:

> We need a radical new Christian inclusion in the Church. This must be grounded in scripture, in reason, in tradition and the Christian faith as the Church of England has received it; it must be based on good, healthy, flourishing relationships, and in *a proper twenty-*

A Lesbian Living in Love and Faith

first century understanding of being human and being sexual.
Inclusion must be radical because the grace of God as expressed in Jesus Christ is radical beyond our imagination. (p. vii, emphasis added)

Here we see an admission that the Church's approach to sexuality and relationships is massively out of step with British society. Quite understandably, they foreground the Anglican emphasis on scripture, tradition and reason; they acknowledge the sensitivities involved; they offer joint apologies for pain inflicted amongst LGBTI people. (Note this anomalous acronym employed in LLF which appears to be unique to LLF.) No formal recommendations are made in this LLF project however. The Bishops seem to be proposing that love and kindness will simply save the day which of course is misguided, fanciful and potentially harmful.

There is an acknowledgment of the Church of England being part of the Worldwide Anglican Communion, thus exacerbating the foolish wish that we can move on from this debate. I see this as a huge pitfall. If we aim to enter into this listening project spellbound by fear of the Anglican Communion's reactions there will never be any genuine liberation for LGBTQ+ people in the Church of England. We need to be honest about this. Homosexuality remains illegal in 40 Commonwealth countries. The Archbishop of Nigeria, the Most Revd Henry Ndukuba, recently claimed that homosexuality is a "deadly virus" (*Church Times*, 2021). Further, in an African Youth Survey conducted last year in 14 African countries 69% disagreed with the statement "My country should do more to protect the rights of LGBTQ people" (Economist, 2021, 45). Is the Church of England going to continue to collude with such manic and murderous homophobia?

"The aim of this project", the Bishops explain, "is to learn and reflect together to help the entire church in its task of discernment". Their vision, they hope, citing Jesus's farewell speech (John 17:21) is that the Church will be one. They admit that they recognise that being one is not synonymous with sameness. *So what is it?*

Hypocrisy between teaching and reality

The tone in the book is largely open and considered, mostly erring on the side of bland. The desire to be measured is more than evident. Thankfully, divergence of opinion is admitted in some places, allowing us to recognize how polarised the church is today. In the chapter on Religion, the Bishops' document, *Issues on Human Sexuality*, is introduced. The decision that was then made that bishops would "*stand alongside......*homophile' faithful relationships is highlighted, as is the agreement that faithful same sex relationships are not permitted for gay clergy. (p. 142). This is swiftly followed however with the caveat that Bishops "did not think it right to interrogate individuals on their sexual lives". (Human Sexuality, 1991) paragraphs 5.13 and 5.22. We are reminded here that the laboured language surrounding homosexuality in general and gay clergy in particular is all at once fudged, veiled and sinister.

As an ordinand and priest my long-term lesbian relationship was dexterously ignored but I am pleased to say that my current experience is more positive though this is certainly not the case for clergy in other dioceses. Bishops in my diocese are aware of my relationship and I have written openly about my sexuality elsewhere (Hogan, 2016). If I were to be told that I should not have a sexual relationship with my partner I would, without doubt, but with profound sadness, resign my orders. To be affirmed with one breath that I can count my lesbian relationship as acceptable by the Church, yet rejected when the desire I have for my partner is expressed sexually is absurd. It is unarguable that there is a profound dissonance between what is formally agreed in synod and what is blessed in practice.

Everyone knows that sexuality, relationships and gender are complex and freighted with shame and anxiety. It is evident that the creators of LLF admit that this project will hurt and is likely to be difficult for many. And yet, it is highly likely that this may hurt some people more than it will others. For instance, the Pastoral Principles that are applied, identify 'six pervasive evils'. These are explained in an online film with emphatic clarity. That said, it did not augur well for me that a heavy emphasis was being laid on what may easily amount to *being nice*. It reminded me of the nurse in hospital being suspiciously sweet to me moments before undergoing a gruesome procedure. The principle of 'casting out fear' disturbed me the most. *Who*, I asked myself, is the most afraid here? Moreover, recognizing and accepting fear is both necessary and important. In the first podcast there is a discussion inviting everyone involved in LLF "to become vulnerable". Whilst this may sound honest and indeed hopeful, it is important to be aware of and awake to the reality that in this context some people are more vulnerable than others.

In addition to the Pastoral Principles another important starting point is the affirmation that we are all made in the image of God. Certainly, the distinctiveness of this claim is integral to Christianity. Rowan Williams, with characteristic beauty and nuance, writes in his most recent publication about the invitation for us to be visionaries: "Our identity as Christians is to be in the place where Jesus stands, the place from which we can see into the *boundless reality that is the outpouring of God's life*"(Williams, 2020, p. 33). It is this notion of "boundless reality" which identifies the sheer openness and staggering multiplicity of God's creation. Such a wide and varied scope is an invitation to engage constructively in difference, strangeness and otherness.

A strong emphasis here on the doctrine of the *imago dei* is unsurprising because it can be employed as the great equaliser. However, we are not called to accept that we are all the same, but rather as deeply mysterious as the Divine godhead. Managing, through Jesus, to see the Other as the same is not an achievement, but a failure of imagination and insight. Moreover, it is naïve, dishonest and dangerous to presume that achieving sameness in the quest for equality is a worthy goal, not least because it narrows the scope of God's saving acts of love.

Through a feminist lens

As a feminist I question presumptions about gender and reject facile gender binaries. The *fact* remains though that I am female in a world that is ineluctably and tirelessly dominated by male power. Living as a woman within a patriarchy requires that I be not only alert to the particular ways in which I experience the world, but also aware of *how* I am experienced. My female gender in all its myriad and fluid manifestations is my alpha and omega. I wish it was not this way. As a baptised person, Jesus Christ should be the alpha and omega of every breath I take, but the Church and the fallen world which tirelessly privilege masculinity and the male sex at every turn, require me to adopt this particular approach. It is notable that the term 'Misogyny' appears to be absent in the resources, including the glossary, as is the word 'Patriarchy', proof indeed that the Church remains blind to and ill-at-ease with female gender and sexuality.

A Lesbian Living in Love and Faith

Fear of sex talk with God talk

There are further conspicuous absences. For instance, there is little discussion of physical sexual acts as well as the pleasurable experience of making love. It is unsurprising in this context, but it is disappointing nevertheless and reveals the latent and manifest shame the Church continues to experience regarding the body which after all is the locus of erotic desire. It is important to be honest and recognize that there are many people in the Church who are disgusted at the thought of men having sex with men, and there are many people who are either titillated by the idea of women having sex with women, or confused by the idea of lesbian sex. The scant appearance of lesbians across all LLF resources seems to reveal that lesbians are seen as a threat and a mystery.

In the sixteen 'story films' there is only one lesbian couple interviewed (one of whom was barred from ordination owing to her sexuality); yet five films feature gay men. One, an ordinand, speaks about being gay and his decision to be single rather than be in a gay relationship. Interpreting his particular use of language it appears from his narrative that he believes that the Bible does not promote homosexuality so he made the sacrificial choice of God at the expense of a relationship with a man. There is no doubt that celibacy is a gift and a calling, and this is discussed in the book (238ff). However, the decision to be abstinent because of one's sexual orientation should not be conflated with celibacy. Such an approach reinforces the delusion that choosing to refrain from genital physical contact keeps a person 'clean' and therefore eligible for ordination. Some may feel uncomfortable discussing genitals and physical desire but it is precisely this lacuna that has the potential to do great damage. Rowan Williams's assertion in his seminal essay 'The Body's Grace' is that any debate about sexuality is "doomed" because "nothing will stop sex being tragic and comic. It is above all the area of our lives where we can be rejected in our bodily entirety."(Williams, 2000, 324). It appears that LLF recognizes this and yet loses its nerve.

However, the sixteen podcasts reveal that those involved in LLF have thought boldly and imaginatively. Speakers are erudite, experienced and eloquent. The depth and breadth of topics broached shows the Church thinking openly about gender and sexuality more than ever before. Yet some podcasts I listened to discomforted me because a disturbing lack of transparency pervades some of them. For instance, I noted in one conversation that no one spoke explicitly about their views on homosexuality or gender; everything seemed coded. I attempted carefully to de-code their language. Ultimately judgement, dressed up in the form of 'let's try and talk about being open and non-judgemental Christians', is buoyed by vacuous platitudes such as us all being 'Bible believing Christians' which should enable us to manage our perceived differences. What does it mean for us all to *believe in the Bible?* As a lesbian I interpret this statement to mean that some believe that certain people do not read the Bible properly. This coded language is not only dangerous, it is stealthy and dishonest. In another podcast, 'How do we live together?', one contributor, when asked what change he hoped LLF would make replied, "My hope is that the many people I have encountered who have what I would call instincts in one way or another, and not thought them through, would grapple with the scripture and work out what the Bible really says about it". The innocent pronoun 'it' masks the disdain he feels towards LGBTQ+ Christians; 'instincts' I interpret to mean 'homosexual desire'; 'grappling with scripture' I decipher as 'face the facts that the Bible says that being gay is incontrovertibly sinful.' It is this kind of obfuscated language that does deep and sometimes devastating damage. Evangelicals in the Church have vigorously mastered this type of rhetoric and wreaked havoc.

Fear of queer

In addition to being a lesbian I embrace the term queer as an identifying category because it offers a way of resisting social conventions constructed by heterosexual men. A queer life such as mine is one where virtually all normativity is interrogated. I have noticed a conspicuous absence of the term queer in the entire LLF resources. Admittedly, we are warned of this in the 'note to the reader' but there is no explanation of why it has been excluded. The term queer is included in the glossary; here the authors accept that that there is a "growing body of literature" (p. 427) on Queer Theory and Queer Theology. A question should be raised about how and why the decision was made to exclude queer identities in this project. Perhaps queer is viewed as an overtly political term which it is, or deemed too academic which patronizes the reader, thus revealing further patriarchal traces.

The absence of queer further reveals a pernicious preference for niceness which pervades LLF. It is important to note here that the term queer and indeed the verb 'queering' is ineluctably connected to rupture. Queer unsettles, probes, and demands nuance. Queering is a discipline and a way of being. Theologian and priest Elizabeth Edman passionately argues that queer identity "comes to life in community" (Edman, 2014, 93). It is unfortunate that that queer Christian communities have been excluded from this project. Their acuity and energy could have brought enormous insight to this project. The absence of queer theology precludes creative Christological approaches which could enrich discussion. For instance, Jesus' outrage, combined with his resistance to binaries and his preference for a community life not predicated on patriarchal familial structures, is inspirational to queer Christians. Jesus is queer. Queer love, which is dynamic, surpassing gender and sexuality, is revealed in the transgressive Christ who sets me free.

Marriage appears early in the LLF book, signalling its importance in this project. I am unsettled but unsurprised by the emphasis on heterosexual marriage. LLF is in truth an attempt to move forward in the debate about whether LGBTI people can be married in church. I welcomed civil partnership when the Labour government introduced it in 2004; I view this as a sign of justice and I am civilly partnered myself. My partner and I do not wish to be married because we view it as a patriarchal concept and we reject heteronormativity. Two pivotal passages are conspicuously absent, 1 Corinthians 14.32-35 where women are instructed to be subordinate to men and, Ephesians 5.22-24, where women are instructed to obey their husbands. These omissions highlight a failure to face the potentially unsettling misogynistic antecedents of marriage. I recognize that some LGBTQ+ people long to be married in church and I sincerely hope they will be. However, my relationship with my partner is rooted in mutuality and bears all the hallmarks of a healthy, lifegiving and loving relationship without the symbolic and systemic patriarchal constraints.

Clear statements are made in the book regarding same-sex marriage:

> "Some of us maintain – in line with the Church of England's teaching in this area- that marriage between a man and a woman is the only proper context for a sexual relationship" (p. 256).

In the name of fairness, an alternative approach to relationships is offered:

"Some of us say that the critical point in a relationship is where the couple have committed themselves to a lifelong relationship of marriage, and that this promise to be with and for each other and for whatever children come from their union, is the point at which sexual intercourse becomes a fully responsible act of love" (256).

This is a long and convoluted sentence. It is notable that it does not include gender and appears to be suggesting that marriage and procreation need not be the *sine qua non* of a life shared with a person one loves. However, it is the former view that has the upper hand because it is explicitly stated that their view of marriage is "in line with the Church's teaching".

Sexuality is a much more central element of our selfhood than the Church can bear to face. This tendency toward compartmentalisation lies at the root of the profound unease regarding sex and sexuality in the Church. To be alive is to be sexual, however uncomfortable this may sometimes be. As a psychotherapist I believe that a person's desire cannot be restricted to a mechanistic sexual act. Sexuality is what makes us feel alive and indeed it is this precious and powerful gift that is squandered and abused by many. The delight my partner and I have for one another unarguably contributes to who I am as a child of God made in God's image.

Conclusion

Despite the discomfort and frustration I experienced I am pleased to have investigated the LLF resources. There are many elements within LLF which reveal a fervent desire for unity and change. However, I am afraid that such hope is likely to be dashed. There are many intransigent Evangelical Church members whose biblical exegesis is so "violent" (Jennings 2015,p. 210) such that LGBTQ+ people are unlikely to be loved and offered hospitality. A dishonesty and naivete surrounds some of the aims of the LLF project. As a lesbian Christian and priest I am already quite vulnerable in the Church. I resist being a specimen in LLF conversations in the hope of dislodging the scales from some people's eyes. The Church's official teaching and the lively reality of the living body of Christ in communities - *thankfully* in my experience - do not align. The question remains however: can such ambivalence be borne both as a Church and by individuals? Despite commendable efforts I fear that the Bishops' desire for the Church to be one following LLF will not be fulfilled here and many may get hurt in the process. It may just be enough, for now at least, for us to be one through baptism. It is crucial to remember after all that our true end is to desire God above everything else.

Jennie Hogan is Chaplain of Goodenough College London, and a professional psychotherapist

References

Church of England., *Issues in Human Sexuality*. Church House Publishing, 1991.
Edman, E. M. 2016, *Queer Virtue*. Massachusetts: Beacon Press.
Hogan, Jennie, 2017, *This is My Body: A Story of Sickness and Health*. Norwich: Canterbury Press.
Jennings, Theodore W., 2015, "Same-sex relations in the New Testament world". In A. A.Thatcher, ed. *The Oxford Handbook of Theology, Sexuality and Gender*. Oxford: Oxford University Press. pp. 206-221.
Rowan Williams, 2020, *Candles in the Dark :Faith, Hope and Love in a Time of Pandemic*. London: SPCK.
Rowan Williams, 2002, "The Body's grace". In *Theology and Sexuality*, E. F. Rogers ed. Oxford: Blackwell. pp. 309-322. *The Economist*, March 12-16, 2021.
The *Church Times*, accessed 12 March 2021.

Now You See Us, Now You Don't

A Trans Perspective on LLF

RACHEL MANN

It has become *de rigeur* for speakers at General Synod to begin their speeches with declarations of interest, signalling either expertise or ways in which their contribution is compromised. In that spirit, I should declare an interest. I was not a member of either the Living in Love and Faith (LLF) Co-ordinating Group or the working parties which generated the LLF materials.[1] However, I am a member of the Faith and Order Commission (FAOC). I, along with colleagues, was given sight of various drafts of the final book, and I was able to offer shaping comments.

I want, then, to acknowledge my involvement, however tangentially, in the latest iteration of the Church of England's ever messy and complex wrangling over sexuality, gender identity and relationships. I also want to acknowledge that, for the first time, I sense theological promise in what the Church of England – that ever elusive (set of) institution(s) – is up to regarding human identity. For the first time, through the work of LLF, the Church acknowledges the complexity, richness and messiness of personhood, desire and embodiment. Indeed, trans identities are present as more than glancing references or 'sidebars'. I'm less sure whether trans people are yet fully recognised in the LLF materials as persons with equal dignity as non-trans people. However, as I stated to FAOC colleagues in September 2019, LLF offers a fresh way to do theological work in the Church of England.

This article sets out with a modest aim. Firstly, I shall attempt to offer an overview of the places where questions of gender identity become significant focal points in the main LLF book resource; secondly, I shall indicate where there is real strength or points of insight in the material and, finally, I shall reflect on areas of weakness or missed opportunity.

At whom is this resource aimed?

I begin with this question because it will help me delineate what a rigorous, but generous reading of the LLF material might look like. An appreciation of intended audience and writing level will enable me to offer a nuanced response, rather than simply excoriate for its failure to be something it never intended to be.

The Invitation made at the beginning of the LLF book states this: 'We, the Bishops of the Church of England, invite you to join us in using this book and its accompanying resources to learn together about how the Christian understanding of God relates to questions of identity, sexuality, relationships and marriage' (1). They add, 'Our prayer is that as all of us, the people of God, take time to listen and learn together, our love for one another will be deepened and our faith in Jesus Christ strengthened …' (1). It is clear, then, that the College of Bishops (operating out of the principle that bishops lead the Church) intend the 'you' of the opening sentence to mean 'all of us'. LLF is seen less as a 'teaching document' from the Bishops and more as a learning resource and 'journey' with the purpose of inviting all, including the Bishops themselves, to participate in the transforming Love of Jesus Christ.

A learning resource intended for 'all' cannot be an academic treatise. Indeed, it was reported to me by a PhD researcher who attended a Chester Theological Society study event on LLF held on 21st February 2021, that Mark Tanner (Bishop of Chester and a former theological educator) suggested that the LLF book is pitched at about an 'A Level'. While pitching a book at 'A Level' inevitably means that some in the category 'all of us' will be excluded, this should, perhaps, not cause undue concern; rather it helpfully delineates the relative sophistication of the LLF book. Equally, LLF is not just the book. It is a suite of resources, including a five-week course pitched as genuinely open access.[2]

However, before evaluating the 'trans content' of LLF, there is one anecdotal 'sidebar' I hope will give us pause should we wish unthinkingly to accept the Bishops' claim that these resources are aimed at 'all of us'. It centres on this question: Who exactly is included (and potentially excluded) in the word 'all'? The answer may seem obvious, but recent socio-political movements like 'Black Lives Matter' have drawn attention to the way 'all' can be a weasel word. The phrase 'All Lives Matter' has sometimes been offered as a counter to #BLM; more often than not it has been used in a way that, ironically, erases the facts of black lives for the sake of a white majority uncomfortable with attention being centred on black and brown bodies.[3] 'All' can be a way of reinscribing the power of those who already possess it.

My anecdote highlights the dangers about uncritically speaking of 'all' or 'all of us'. At General Synod in July 2019 I attended presentations laid by the working groups preparing the LLF material. One session I attended was presented by Professor Chris Cook, a psychiatrist and academic at Durham University. He gave an overview on trans, non-binary and intersex identities from a primarily socio-scientific perspective. It was a solid presentation which has formed the basis for the LLF book content on trans, non-binary and intersex people. The information shared was, in my view, essentially accurate. However, the tone was curious.

As Chris spoke, he gave his presentation in the register of 'us' and 'them'. He spoke to the Synod delegates as if trans, non-binary or intersex people were 'out there' and not part of the life of Synod, let alone the Church. Trans people were 'them' not 'us'. I found myself become ever more agitated. The friends I was with – both cis people – shared my sense of alarm.

Perhaps Chris was nervous and his tone was a simple error, a kind of verbal slip. Perhaps he had no idea who I was, as an out trans member of Synod. Perhaps – to cut him some slack – he was *de facto* right to speak of trans people in 'othered' terms. Perhaps, unconsciously, he was revealing the truth: that in the mind of most Synod members and church people, trans people and intersex people are not part of 'all of us'. Certainly, judging from previous C of E reports on identity and sexuality, trans people have barely been present. Equally, while I know that when most Bishops speak of 'all of us' they are sincere in wishing to include LGBT+ people. However, as I hope will become clear, how trans people are included in Church discourse remains problematic.

How does the LLF represent Trans People? Trans People as Social and Medical Phenomena
I want to look now at how trans people appear in the LLF book and examine how the text both treats trans people as social and medical phenomena and constructs its position on us. I want to suggest that LLF is not interested in trans and non-binary people in and of themselves. One way of opening up that claim is by noting LLF's framing devices. The subtitle of the LLF book asserts that it examines 'Christian teaching and learning about identity, sexuality, relationships and marriage.' In its opening chapters, the book frames this learning project in terms of 'gift': firstly, it reminds the reader/learner that human life and identity itself is gift from God. Then, behind that primary reality, comes the assertion that the gift of life should be framed in terms of the gift of relationship. This gift is known between persons and between communities and persons with the Living God. Finally, it offers 'marriage' as a fundamental example of God's gift in relationship. That the book shifts gear from relationships *per se* to marriage in particular is telling; it indicates the central anxiety of this project: that for all the Bishops' desire to frame the conversation in terms of the gift of life and relationship, the real nub is 'marriage'.

If this is not the place to analyse how successfully the writers of LLF achieve the parsing the book's central focus from 'gift of relationship' into 'gift of marriage', what is telling is how trans identities (and LGBTI+ identities more broadly understood) are not, therefore, treated as 'of interest', celebration, and excitement in and of themselves; rather the focus and scope of LLF ultimately comes down to 'How might trans people fit or not fit into what Christians say about the issue at hand, marriage?'

There is, of course, honesty in acknowledging that *a*, if not *the*, key issue for the LLF project is the status of marriage and who has access to it through the offices of the Church. It just seems so unambitious. LLF might have offered a bold vision of the possibilities of theological anthropology. For all the talk of wanting to hear from trans people and create new understanding and comprehension, the Christian doctrine of Marriage is set out as the lodestone for discussion.

Perhaps the assessment above is too bleak or harsh. So, here is some good news: trans people actually appear in the LLF book. If you can hear a certain archness in that statement, please don't ignore the fact that this, in itself, is – for the Church of England – an advance on previous projects. For example, when I, along with at least one other trans person, was interviewed by members of the *Pilling Report* in preparation for their 2013 publication, I had some hope that we'd been heard and might warrant more than a line or two in the final Report. We did not. LLF, by comparison with the *Pilling Report* or 2014's *Pastoral Guidance on Same-Sex Marriage*, is not only fulsome, but rich. The crumbs from the LLF table give one something to chew on, at least.

Textually, trans people and questions about the nature, shape and possibilities of gender identity first come into focus in *Part II: Paying Attention to What is Going On,* in the chapters on *Society* and *Science*. This part represents a serious attempt to bring the energy of practical theology into the Church of England's theological discourse. That is, having set out the frames of reference – gift, relationship, and marriage – LLF brings an openness to the rich cultural contexts in which the Church is set before bringing the theological power of Scripture and Tradition to bear in later sections.

Thus, in the chapter on *Society*, having (quickly) explored trends in sex and relationships in post-industrial 21st century culture, LLF discusses 'identity'. It understands this term as referring to 'a person's deeply rooted sense of themselves' (88). The discussion of gender identity (93-101) – if one frames this in terms of my earlier discussion about 'audience-level' – is by turns reasonable, careful and honest about some of the tensions found in current discourse about trans and non-binary identities. The writers of LLF state that there is no neutral terminology about which to speak of trans people: 'We have chosen to use a set of terms and distinctions that are used in many scientific and academic discussions in this area, and that are important to many trans people ... they are regarded by many trans people as necessary to do justice to their experience' (92).

LLF takes a decision, then, to use descriptors and terms which many (indeed, the vast majority of) trans people cherish and have often established for themselves. This decision I greet warmly. One example of the way LLF is prepared to take trans people seriously is its preparedness to use the word 'cis' to describe 'non-trans' people (95). Equally, the text's analysis of the distinctions between sex and gender, as well as the messiness of the distinctions between the two, represent a genuine step-forward in the Church's discourse on trans people.

There remain aspects in LLF's approach to gender identity which strike me as likely to annoy many trans people. LLF states that every exploration of gender identity is 'theory-laden' (93). I do understand why the writers say this: Some trans people use the work of academics like Judith Butler, Kimberle Crenshaw, Jack Halberstam et al. to give voice to their understanding of themselves. However, in the context of LLF, the phrase seems to act as code for saying that trans identities are disputed in social discourse. There is, according to LLF, no neutral way of talking 'gender'. Certainly, there is a lot of heat – not least on social media – generated about trans lives. However, there is a certain kind of 'even-handed' mendacity about the way LLF frames its discourse about trans people. The truth is, surely, that 'neutrality' in any discourse is problematic. I'm not sure there is a neutral way of talking about sexuality or human identity *per se*; our terminologies always indicate pre-existing commitments to imaginaries, beliefs and positions. There is no 'Rawlsian' outside-of-a-position. Even medical terminology is never merely neutral. So, why draw particular attention to it in the case of 'gender'?

The discussion about trans people in LLF continues in the chapter on *Science* (109-120). As with the analysis in the chapter on *Society*, LLF takes the not unreasonable strategy of being cautious and careful. For example, in the section *The Science of Gender Identity*, LLF states, modestly, that 'the origins and nature of gender identity are currently poorly understood' (109). Equally, when speaking of gender transition and transgender and gender diverse children and adolescents (110-11), LLF adopts a surveying approach. Its discussion of peer-reviewed research on the wellbeing of post-transition trans people leaves the reader to draw an unavoidable conclusion: that a tiny percent of trans people regret transition.

The book's analysis of trans and gender-diverse children and adolescents is less confident. LLF states, 'treatment [using puberty blockers] is controversial'. While this claim holds truth, I should have welcomed more careful framing. LLF ignores the widespread and standardised use of such therapies across the globe and ill-defines among whom such treatment is controversial in the UK. I especially note the weakness of LLF's claim, in relation to gender transition procedures, that, 'while there is evidence of benefit, controversy among some scientists about the risks, morality and therapeutic desirability and effectiveness of these procedures continues' (119). The authors cite one article on support of 'controversy'.

Trans people as a category, then, appear as fully in LLF as they have ever appeared in any Church of England document. It is notable that we do so primarily as a category for discussion: either as social phenomenon or as part of a discussion around contemporary science. When said in such stark terms, I am uncomfortable about how trans people are represented. We are treated, as we have so often been treated, as a category for analysis; as objects for discussion. Our agency and humanity are diminished. If we are included in the category 'all of us' we do so, at best, in the margins.

However, I do not want to be unfair. LLF takes the step of adding the leaven of storytelling to its account/s of human identity. It is to the appearance in LLF of trans people as persons telling their story that I now turn.

How does LLF Represent Trans People? Trans People as Persons with a Story to Tell

The LLF book invites the reader to undertake a series of 'encounters' with actual people's lives. This is in line with the LLF process's commitment to learning together. LLF states, '...stories remind us that we are learning together as a community of disciples ...' (48). The authors add, 'attending to the stories ... has the potential to transform us ... these 'Encounters' are there to drive us deeper into Christ' (49).

Leaving aside the curious idea of being 'driven' into Christ, LLF certainly has the virtue of presenting, without comment, a rich variety of human stories. These include those who decide that sex before marriage is anathema to Christians as well as confident and proud queer couples. It is beyond peradventure that, when added to the video resources also available, LLF presents hitherto undreamed of textures to Christian pictures of human flourishing in relationship.

The 'Encounters' in the book engage with trans people on several occasions. Firstly, we 'appear' as part of a conversation between sixth-form students at a Church of England Academy in the north of England (156). It is unclear whether any of the students is trans, but it is implied that they are not. Here we hear the voices of a small group of young people discussing trans and gay people. While it is good to hear young people wresting with societal norms, it entails, once again trans people being talked about rather than talked to. On p.159 we meet Emma, our first trans person. Emma describes herself as bigender and presents as a woman for the interview. The interview helpfully breaks open fresh vistas on 'trans' identity: Emma shows that being trans doesn't necessarily mean being someone who either intends to transition or has transitioned. The interview is respectful – for example, female pronouns are used throughout – and has the power to challenge conservative ideas about trans identity from both within and without the trans community. Later in the book we meet Jack, a man who had a strong urge to dress in women's clothing as a young person. Through his Christian friends and faith he reached a point where he 'kicked the habit' of cross-dressing. He experienced a sense of freedom from what felt like a trap. Finally, we are introduced to Chloe, who when she was 17 was told by her parents that her dad had gender dysphoria. She talks about the difficulty and pain of processing losing her 'father' and how faith helped her forgive.[4]

There is one further 'encounter'. The book includes an anonymised conversation about gender identity and transition (398). There are five interlocutors, of which one (Gabriel) is trans. The interlocutors were involved in the creation of the book, presumably as part of the Coordinating Group. While the conversation arrives at a generous, eirenic conclusion – 'perhaps ... we are learning that we need to tread really carefully when we talk about these things' (404) – I was concerned by the extent to which one person acted as a representative for trans people in this discussion.

The conversation is framed in terms of medical and ideological concerns: a cis man 'David' asks, 'Can we begin with probing differences between gender dysphoria and gender ideology?' I'm really not sure this is where trans people would begin a conversation about their dignity and reality and it seems to reflect an unconscious desire to understand trans people as either medical or socially constructed categories, again. While Gabriel does a terrific job of shaping the conversation in more human and nuanced ways, I was on the edge of my seat as I first read this conversation. One trans person alone negotiating the privilege of cis people who set the discursive agenda reinscribes all the power imbalances which exist in the Church of England. This cannot be the way forward.

Conclusion: Are We Really Present? Are We Taken Seriously?
Well, trans people are present in LLF and, given LLF's brief to resource the Church, our presence, even through social and scientific categories, should extend the frame of conversation and understanding. While the LLF text runs the risk of treating trans people as adjuncts to the 'serious business', it clearly indicates that trans people are here and we're going nowhere.

My key disappointment with LLF centres on a sense of missed opportunity. The LLF book includes significant sections about the

Bible and the Church, among others. Unless I am much mistaken, these sections on biblical theology and ecclesiology make no substantive references to trans people, except in noting, in the chapter on the Church, legal issues about, for example, whether trans people can be ordained. There is an utterly unambitious approach to exploring the possibilities of the biblical text in relation to gender, whether that be in relation to biblical texts which trans/queer writers have found encouraging or challenging.[5] The biblical texts discussed in LLF fixate on sex and marriage.

Even if I were willing to give LLF a free pass on its lack of interest in trans people/theologians' contributions to biblical analysis, the real issue I think is this: throughout LLF there is no willingness to explore how gender may offer a disruptive prism through which to interrogate presumptions about the nature of sexuality and marriage. Once we accept the reality of trans and non-binary people – as I think LLF is grudgingly willing to do – every Church claim about sexuality, identity, and marriage is surely open to critique. For example, the Church claims that marriage is between one man and one woman. Trans and non-binary people problematise what is meant by that claim, exposing the artificiality and presumed permanence of 'natural' categories like man and woman. I cannot be alone in thinking that, even in a resource aimed at the whole Church, such theological disruptions are not too sophisticated to be wrestled with.

LLF is a project, then, which invites marginal people into the Church's conversation and, finally, leaves us still in the margins. *LLF*, for all its efforts to deploy the techniques of practical theology, never quite acknowledges how power operates in its discourse. The 'Church' refuses to permit trans people, as full members of the Body of Christ, to disrupt the meanings of that Body. The day is surely coming when that will change. Even if it doesn't, I can't see how the Church can flourish without trans people, and other 'marginal' people.

Rachel Mann is the priest of St Nicholas Burnage in the Diocese of Manchester. She is also a poet and author. www.rachelmann.co.uk

Notes

1. There was trans representation on the LLF Co-ordinating Group. Before her resignation, the Rev'd Dr Christina Beardsley was an out trans member. She was replaced with a non-binary URC minister, the Rev'd Alex Clare-Young.
2. It is worth noting that the wider five-week course has a different feel to the book. It works very much on the assumption that a very wide range of people will be able to reflect together with relatively little scriptural, scientific, or theological knowledge.
3. Theological critiques of easy assumptions about who is and who isn't excluded from 'universalising' claims about identity have long been provided by Black, Womanist, Feminist and Queer theologies, to name a few.
4. It is worth noting that the 'suite' of resources also includes a video of a married couple, one of whom is non-binary and the other cis. The videos also include a couple, one of whom is trans, whose position on trans identities is such an outlier that she has been called transphobic. Her inclusion in the suite of resources is likely to be alienating to so many in the trans community that one wonders if her inclusion might be counterproductive to the 'reception' of LLF among trans people.
5. For example, Genesis 1.26-27; Genesis 37.1-4; Galatians 3.28, et al.

—Divorce or New Birth?—

Living in Love and Faith and the Future of the Church of England

ROBERT SONG

A few years ago, in a presentation to a group of Christian leaders, I made an effort to shift the metaphors of the Church of England's current anguish over sexuality. Perhaps what we are currently experiencing, I mused, should be understood not in terms of marriage, as the pain of incipient divorce, but in terms of pregnancy, as the birth pains of something unexpected and new. Warming to my tune, I ventured that we might be moving to a place that none of us had anticipated or imagined – only for my enthusiasm to be punctured by a gruff voice from the audience in response: 'a new birth, yes', they conceded, before adding, 'but it might be twins'.

The Living in Love and Faith process – and it is a process before it is a book or set of resources – may represent the last, best chance the Church of England has of resetting its disputes over identity, sexuality, relationships and marriage. Instead of interminable trench warfare, and the querulous, frustrated and resentful zero-sum game with which we have become familiar, we are being offered the opportunity of something more open, honest, and engaging. Decisively, despite placing themselves in the line of Church of England statements on homosexuality from the Board of Social Responsibility in 1970 to the Pilling Report in 2013, the project's architects have eschewed the traditional format of the Working Party report. Gone are the numbered paragraphs, the summary of recommendations, and the inevitable ensuing General Synod bust-up about whether the report should be approved, noted, or even published at all.

Most importantly, gone is the sense that a small group of bishops and experts can attempt to pronounce on behalf of the church. On the contrary, '[d]iscerning the mind of Christ for the Church is the task of the whole people of God', as they quote the Anglican Communion's 1997 Virginia Report (320). Having myself been involved in what may have been the last hurrah for the Working Party approach to Church of England documents on sexuality, I cannot have been alone in wondering what right ten people sitting round a room in Church House had to say anything on the subject that might have been remotely capable of representing the whole people of God. Quite properly, the first and most important recommendation of the Pilling Group was that these matters should be discussed and owned by the whole Church of England, national and local, through a process of facilitated listening which came to be known as the Shared Conversations.

Living in Love and Faith follows through and richly develops that original impulse, even if it was established only after a circuitous route of episcopal proposition and synodical opposition, the upshot of which was a proposal by the Archbishops for a 'teaching document'. Yet if there was ever a concern that this might be exactly what it sounded like, i.e. the bishops telling the Church what to think, this has been entirely dispelled in the event. Rather than prescribing how the Church should think, what we have in the Living in Love and Faith resources is an extensive description and arrangement of the different ways Christians in the Church of England in fact now think about identity, sexuality, relationships and marriage. As with the *Oxford English Dictionary*, the editorial line is not to act as the arbiter of proper usage, but to depict the Church's actual usage. By laying out the available Biblical and theological tools, the hope goes, the whole people of God will be supported in discerning the mind of Christ.

In so far as a set of resources could ever be up to such a task, taken as a whole they seemed to me exceptionally well judged. Like many, I have found the story films to be particularly compelling. If the book is long, it is no longer than it need be, and sighs from its critics that it might be shorter have not on the whole been matched by proposals about what exactly might have been cut. *Au contraire.* Moreover its style is accessible and freshly written, the tone consistently measured and eirenic – the latter in particular is an extraordinary achievement given the extreme diversity of opinion among the contributors. It wears its scholarship lightly, and rarely references individual theologians or even movements; the reader will be left little the wiser about how Catholic or Reformed (or Augustinian or Thomist or Barthian) it takes itself to be, for example. Its object is much less to single out the faults of those they disagree with than to seek out the virtues, and often the complementary virtues, in each of the positions they identify. There will not be many who do not have plenty to learn from it, not least from what the authors refrain from saying and from their delicate, unsignalled nuances (if, to take one tiny example, there were any occasions when the masculine pronoun was used for God, they escaped this reader).

As much as a teaching document, it is a learning document, and it is gratifying that the bishops repeatedly acknowledge that they too are part of the learning community which they are inviting others to join. More broadly, it is not impossible to imagine that these resources might provide one huge step forward in the long neglected task of Anglican lay and congregational training. There are many well-drilled parts of the Church which already know what they think on identity, sexuality, relationships and marriage. But equally there is a large constituency of lay people whose weekly experience of parish life typically tells them little or nothing of the seething antagonisms that threaten the national Church and the Anglican Communion. For them the opportunities offered by this process are welcome. Anything is to be applauded which lowers the barriers to understanding, removes the daunting aura of expertise which Bible study and theology is thought to require, allows people to articulate their inchoate instincts, and enables them to find their views recognised and respected. An increasingly confident laity, engaged with Biblical and theological thinking, could speak words of truth into the Church's conversation in accordance with the 'Pentecost principle' (321) of Acts 2.18, that God can speak through any believer, whatever their gender or social or ecclesiastical status.

All of this keeps alive the hope that the Church might move to a place that none of us had expected or imagined. The question follows whether the book itself bears any indication of what that place might look like. To be sure, its main concern has been to describe rather than to take sides, a promise which has probably kept the warring parties engaged in the process, even as they also find themselves infuriated that it means yet further delay. Yet while a merely descriptive exercise cannot determine specific normative conclusions (in this sense no 'ought' can be derived from an 'is'), equally it would be naïve to think that there is any such thing as 'mere' description either.

Take the example of their handling of the question of how the Bible provides authoritative answers to our concerns (294-309). They imagine a panel of speakers, each representing a theological position on a range from 1, which for shorthand could be labelled an extreme 'conservative' stance, to 7 at the 'liberal' extreme. Positions 1 and 7 are soon ruled out as being 'beyond the mainstream of the church's conversation' (298), denying the roles respectively of human beings and of God in the authorship of Scripture. Those positions are no doubt to be found around the Church, but evidently not anything goes, even in a descriptive exercise. However it is their handling of speakers 5 and 6 which is particularly interesting. By contrast with speakers 2 and 3, who might regard themselves as representing a 'high' view of Scripture, sitting under its authority, and seeking to be obedient to its 'plain' teaching, speakers 5 and 6 emphasise the centrality of love in the Bible's message, in the latter case arguing that the Bible is given 'for the one purpose of teaching us about God's love for the world' (296), everything else in Scripture needing to be tested against that message.

Against the suggestion that only speakers 2 and 3 take the Bible seriously, it is argued that all of the speakers share much in common: a commitment to holiness, to diligent reading of Scripture, to being formed by Scripture, to the centrality of Christ, and so on. All of them are committed to the authority of Scripture, but disagree about what that authority consists in. But aren't speakers 5 and especially 6 setting themselves up over against Scripture, by suggesting that some parts of Scripture are not authoritative for us? Not so, it is suggested, since they are continuing a process of commentary and critique that one finds going on in the Bible itself, between the New and Old Testaments, and indeed within each of them. But doesn't this imply sitting light to the consistency and reliability of Scripture? Not necessarily, perhaps, since it is also being true to the Bible we actually have been given to attend to. And so it goes.

The result, in disagreements over both the authority of Scripture and the nature of its central message, turns out to be a score draw. They observe, in lieu of a conclusion, that 'the kinds of differences that we have been exploring have proven – over decades of intense debate – resistant to being overcome by argument' (302). And when they turn to how each of the speakers' positions matches up against the Church of England's sources of authority, the result comes out the same. Article 20 may state that 'it is not lawful for the Church to ordain any thing that is contrary to God's Word written', and that we should not 'expound one place of Scripture that it be repugnant to another', but speaker 6 apparently might respond that by allowing the central message of love to govern their interpretation of all of Scripture, by definition they cannot be interpreting it in a way that is internally contradictory. And the situation is no different at the global level: Anglican Communion pronouncements on the nature and authority of Scripture have at times veered to the conservative, sometimes to the liberal. But the 'more normal' pattern has been 'an affirmation of the unique authority of Scripture, without any clear ruling on what kinds of approach to Scripture this affirmation rules out' (308).

I happen to be very sympathetic to the place they reach, in terms of their rejection of the idea that to emphasise the decisive centrality of God's love in Christ is somehow unAnglican or unChristian. But in the context of the current state of play in the Church of England, it is hard not to read this as a rather robust resourcing of the speakers 5 and 6 end of the argument. Over against the well-advertised claims of those at the other end to be the only ones adhering to the supreme authority of Scripture, it represents something of a levelling up of the playing field. To be sure, the authors do not underestimate the depth and intractibility of the disagreements at stake: after their three years in conclave, who could begrudge them that recognition? And they are clear that there is no pre-ordained trajectory towards an 'agree to disagree' goal: '[w]e have not tried to provide a recipe for discernment,' as they conclude Part Four, 'but instead to map its various dimensions' (367). Yet from now on it will be easier for those who are not sure that the lineaments of their faith have been quite caught by more conservative styles of thinking to think that their views have some measure of theological validation.

The nature and authority of the Bible is not the only point where one could reach the conclusion that there is a certain degree of levelling going on. On the relationship between church and culture, where one group is accused of sectarianism, and the other of capitulation to worldly standards, they argue that both groups 'are seeking to be faithful to Christian truth – but they disagree about the proper understanding of that truth' (351): where one sees cultural ideas that are opposed to the gospel, the other finds from the culture a way into a deeper understanding of the gospel. On sin, the disagreements are not between those who take sin seriously and those who do not. On identity, the disagreements are not 'between those who are and those who are not convinced that their deepest identity is in Christ' (217). Nor are the conservatives the only ones who are subject to misconceptions. On dignity, the disagreements are not between those who recognize the equal dignity of all, and those who do not; and on diversity, the differences are not between those who celebrate human diversity and those who do not. In every case there are different understandings of different aspects of human experience at stake, and not – or not only – intellectual, moral or spiritual obtuseness.

In each of these, their judgements found a broadly well-disposed audience in this reader. But judgements they are, and not the simple report of a debate. And if they are judgements, they must have been made in accordance with some set of criteria, even if those criteria remain tacit, obscure or or even incoherent.

One of those criteria, we should be clear, is simply one of intellectual charity. Some of what I have described as a 'levelling' arises from the effort to ensure that every position they represent is given its most favourable hearing, and not simply the spin offered by its opponents: in some cases perhaps that required supplying argumentation where they perceived deficiency.

But this principle of charity, while itself in one sense a formal or procedural principle, may also point rather more substantially and materially towards how they envisage the future of the Church. Whether they intend it or not, by refusing to delegitimise certain approaches to the authority of Scripture, by recognising that there is value on both sides of the debate on church and culture, by taking accommodating positions on the issues of identity, dignity, and so on, they have implicitly staked out an account of what the Church could be. Indeed if one asks what is Anglican about Living in Love and Faith, or if one asks for a report on what Anglicanism now is, as received in the Church of England, it might be precisely an acknowledgement of a conscious plurality, marked by a spirit of interpretive charity, and – crucially – centred on a generous orthodoxy. A church defined by geographical location, whose origins lie at least as much in political fiat as in doctrinal dispute, which bears the scars of its turbulent history, now could be seen to prize the ability to articulate difference rather than to impose doctrinal uniformity as one mark of its identity – as if the one Spirit is honoured in the first place not through standardisation of belief, but through a shared discernment together of the truth, the first step towards which is the truthful delineation of difference.

Divorce or New Birth?

To affirm this is not to endorse indifference to, or denial of the possibility of, truth, of course: an honest confession of disagreement is *not* the same as relativism. Nor is it the same as saying that this kind of capaciousness could be tolerated on any doctrinal matter. Here the book's analysis of three different levels of disagreement and their relation to communion is sharp: they distinguish (i) disagreements where each group regards the other as compromising the gospel itself from (ii) those which make it difficult to work together as one church, and (iii) those which are serious but don't prevent working together in the church, and rightly note that in the current disputes there is no agreement about which level the disagreement is at. At all events, accepting disagreement here does not mean accepting disagreement everywhere. Nor, finally, does it mean that episcopal and synodical decisions will not have to be taken soon, decisions which cannot be held off forever.

Of course, there is much more to be said on the substance of the book. For myself, I wonder whether, in addition to describing the many areas of disagreement they cover, there could have been room for explicit, thickly described accounts of the visions of the good that different participants in the debate have. Though not myself conservative on this, I do think conservatives have struggled to articulate how the gospel can represent an imaginative and attractive vision for LGBTI+ people's lives. While some of the most distressing testimonies scattered throughout the materials came from LGBTI+ people in conservative churches, some of the most striking stories came from there as well, and this could have been an excellent opportunity to take it much further.

Another lack is a closer look at the history of marriage in the Christian tradition. Chapter 3 contains an account of the Biblical and liturgical basis of the Christian understanding of marriage 'as the Church of England has received it' (24), but its fifteen pages left one assuming that a rather fuller account of the historical and theological changes in the Christian teaching on marriage was to come. The natural place for this would have been in chapter 14, on the Church; but, unlike chapter 13 which included both an overview of the principles of interpreting Scripture and an account of several central Biblical texts on sexuality, gender and marriage, the chapter on the Church discusses the principles of 'listening to the tradition', with barely a reference to the substance of the topics at hand. Consequently the reader is left underequipped to come to a judgement whether the

Divorce or New Birth?

changes that have happened are changes to the core, essential doctrine of marriage, or to contingent, accidental features of it.

One change in the doctrine of marriage which has a good claim to be regarded as a change in its essence, rather than just its contingent features, concerns the teaching on contraception, a matter whose significance is rather glossed over in the two places where they discuss the Anglican Communion's departure from the Western tradition precipitated by the 1930 Lambeth Conference. By contrast, its significance was not lost on Pope Pius XI, whose encyclical *Casti Connubii*, defending the prohibition on artificial contraception, was rushed out in response, nor on the generations of conservative Catholic apologists who have rightly argued that once the connection between sex and procreation has been deliberately severed, especially if that is for the duration of a marriage, then it is unclear why marriages need to be heterosexual. Of course, those many Anglicans who happily endorse contraception for the entirety of a marriage and are incredulous that the Church of England may ever have thought anything different, let alone so recently, may not think that this is the implication of what they are doing. But the facts have been made on the ground for the best part of a century now, and it is not too early to begin some theological reflection on their implications.

One way of pursuing that theological reflection might be as follows. Sexual ethics is connected to creation, as the authors rightly note, but they arguably do not offer an integrated theological account of how creation is ordered to its eschatological fulfilment in Christ, leaving the whole inadequately Christological. The orientation of marriage to procreation is resituated in a situation where Christians reproduce by baptism and not birth, and it may be that the logic of this points to a reordering of marriage even in this time between the times, such that childless but otherwise fruitful marriage becomes a theologically intelligible good. The significance of this for our understanding of gender would be profound: sexual differentiation ('male and female he created them' (Gen. 1.27)) remains a good because having children remains a good (to deny which would tend towards Gnosticism), *but simultaneously* sexual differentiation has been superseded ('no longer male and female' (Gal.3.28)) because having children is no longer essential for Christian fulfilment.

Not all of these matters could reasonably have been included within the terms of the Living in Love and Faith project. But it is to its huge credit that the Church is being enabled to have the kind of discussions where over time they could begin to be held up for scrutiny. Communities are formed not only by their shared agreements, as is often suggested, but also by their willingness to get on despite their disagreements. If Living in Love and Faith were only to enable that recognition, then if our current travails were to give birth to twins, their names would not be 'liberal' and 'conservative', but 'agreeing to disagree' and 'not agreeing to disagree'.

Robert Song is Professor of Theological Ethics at Durham University

— **Forum** —

Cathedrals and the 'Science' of Innovation: Reflecting on a Coastal Micro-Initiative

FRANCIS DAVIS

It is not surprising that some have called for a need for a 'science' of Cathedral studies.[1] Very often with greater footfall than any megachurch on either side of the Atlantic Cathedrals, Shrines and Abbeys act as crucial economic and civic 'anchor institutions' and sustain myriad initiatives focused on social inclusion.[2] In these places the materiality and the idea of the 'institution' of the Cathedral interplay with imagination, place, relationships and reach to unlock significant public value.

This article reflects on the impact of one award winning initiative namely the *Cathedral Innovation Centre* (CIC) based in and from the sea - side Anglican Cathedral of Portsmouth.

Portsmouth 2012: Jobs Needed

Portsmouth is the most densely populated city in the UK. Many of its wards match the most stretched for poverty. In the period running up to 2013 maths attainment in schools was among the weakest nationally. Local social need is also complicated by a heavier concentration than most areas of residents in the city and adjoining towns living after military service with its distinctive effects on psychological, family and employment prospects.

Once described by *The Observer* as 'the Burnley of the South' Portsmouth has traditionally also had an economy that has relied disproportionately on significant public spending; That spending had dropped via cuts to the Naval Docks and Royal Naval Headquarters

Forum

in the later years of Blair/Brown Labour. Post 2010 the financial conservatism of the Coalition government was working its way through to the frontline. Where were the new jobs going to come from especially for those who were at the bottom of the economic pyramid or, like me, who had experienced a 'life course disruption'?

From Carer to Innovator

Canon Nick Ralph and I bumped in to each other in Old Portsmouth. We had long been debating how the Church's theory of social change advocating trickle-down Keynesian policy levers of bureaucratic Whitehall was a 'busted flush'.[3]

He was walking towards a meeting of the Cathedral property committee lamenting that it had been impossible to find tenants for the ground floor of Cathedral House and how little used the space was. A spark: I suggested a Cathedral Innovation Centre and we started to buzz. Little did we know that that moment would define thousands of hours of my volunteer time over the coming seven years.[4]

A Model not a Document

The aim of the Cathedral Innovation Centre was focused intensely on job creation and rooted in a conviction that jobs are best created when firms are launched, grow and succeed. Reports from Church House and the like were all well and good but enterprise was not some far away conceptual capitalism but in our vision a mode of agency, participation and inclusion not least for those who sought to 'begin' or 'begin again'. I got to work.[5]

Everyone who contacted us we met and talked through their needs: One student wanted us to pay her £25000 per annum for three years so there would be no risk to her in setting up a fashion firm. No thanks. A young designer needed help because as his practice grew the time to do paperwork was getting later and later at night. A tech start up needed a Non - Executive Director while two women making ethical home furnishings needed an address as the attic from which they worked was now full. Yes please. As we met people across the sectors, age groups and ranges of hope, we developed an offer rooted deeply in the 'gift relationships' that Cathedrals embody and which gather about them.

A Mutual Ethic

Each venture's 'support package' was tailor-made to the public value they would unlock, the stage of their business development and their potential. Office costs would be lower for those creating jobs, back office and marketing support would be at nil cost to those with very strong social purposes. Great attention was paid to building synergies between the ventures linked to the CIC..

We recruited business mentors from the Cathedral congregation but also from across the Anglican Diocese. The local Catholic Cathedral joined but soon wider civic allies saw the potential. We established a partnership with accounting students from the local Business School. Under supervision they could gain academic credit by doing the accounts and audit for our increasing number of 'ventures in residence'. Awarded 'Catalyst' status by the Royal Society of Arts I appealed for volunteers through the RSA's regional Fellowship. Former military Officers and board directors, FE leaders and the CEO of a Local Economic Partnership, equity investors and pro bono business advisors all came forward.[6]

Local parishes offered free storage for ventures that were making products, others meeting space and others would simply buy products and services and recommend the fledgling firms. The then Dean would make a point, for example at the annual civic service, of introducing start-ups to local leaders with procurement budgets (so 'saving years of networking and banging on closed doors'). [7]

The local business pages took interest. Radio 4 *In Business*[8] came to visit as did *Sunday* Programme and ITV. The local MPs, Flick Drummond and Penny Mordaunt were incredibly supportive. Working with the local university we created two full fees *'Cathedral Innovation Centre Scholarships'* with an in-kind value of £40,000 on the Portsmouth MBA for innovators in education and tech[9] Working nationally we championed access to business start- up loans for faith based social enterprises.[10]

For a legal form we chose mutuality. This enabled us to launch a community share offer attracting around £17,000 in £1 shares sold in multiples of £75. The Centre was *of* the Cathedral, *because* of the Cathedral but *not owned by* the Cathedral. It was a co-operative.

The Cathedral Chapter modelled partnership in this regard – acting as convenor and servant and this brought further civic dividends: Working with the think tank *Theos* and the participation charity *Involve* in the run up to the 2015 general election I invented *People*

Forum

Inspired which enabled Cathedrals across the UK to convene civic summits to explore unmet and pressing social and economic needs in their regions. Lichfield's was packed, Portsmouth's busy and others followed suit. [11]

In the Diocese of Chelmsford, we provided board members, seed funds and an accounting function to Sophia Hubs which turned a parish building into a start-up and job training centre. In Derby we supported St Peter's Church to turn part of its parish buildings into an Innovation Centre directly inspired by ours. The South East Local Enterprise Partnership covering Essex, East Sussex and Kent asked for help in developing their hopes to be a leading centre of social enterprise.[12]

This request fed into a strategy document that I prepared and was launched by the Civil Society Minister in Whitehall. This strategic contribution to small business development helped shape the LEP's subsequent approach to the use of European Social Funds and their replacement. The publication was subsequently harnessed by the CIC's partners to successfully lobby for a full social enterprise programme at the Solent Local Economic Enterprise Partnership and helped shape subsequent work leading to Cornwall LEP's commitments around inclusive growth.

We ran training workshops for visiting Danish local authority leaders, for Vietnamese Civil Servants and in the private offices of UK Departments of State.

Today we value the in - kind cash, time, space and skills resources unlocked by the Cathedral Innovation Centre and its outreach in excess of £3.5 million. In addition it has attracted at least £4.9 million in investment to its start-up and growth ventures. In excess of 5000 people have attended its training, education and network development meetings. A further 1000 people have visited the Cathedral itself often for the first time. 9 apprenticeships have been created leading to enduring employment and over 125 jobs in over 40 ventures and in three countries. This has been achieved with no government funding.

Failures and Successes: Local and Global

Some ventures could not find adequate sales. A successful digital venture blew up because the friendship of the two founders unravelled. But conference and property companies, accounting and sports firms, finance providers and marine businesses, digital games

Forum

and environmental businesses have all flourished.

Our support helped create and launch the *Hampshire Festival of the Mind*, the *National Mental Wealth Festival*, the Portsmouth Sail Training Trust, a Dial A Ride scheme and a string of start-ups led by those starting again after divorce, major illness, redundancy or trauma. We have been home to the *Good Mental Health Co-operative* and a consultancy that has undertaken major projects for universities at home and abroad. *Street* UK has leant hundreds of thousands in micro loans. For two years we ran an office donated by the FE college in Southampton which in turn created apprenticeships and jobs in addition to those listed above. Again, and again the work has had impact globally but taken on wider directions. Four cases serve as exemplars:

Power2 Inspire[13]

Led by John Willis, a social entrepreneur born without arms and legs, it focuses on mobilising cross community conversations through the shared practice of sport – able bodied and disabled bodied together. Willis launched the charity by undertaking the swim leg of a full triathlon at Eton Dorney Lake before swimming 50 miles in 50 pools giving 50 talks in 50 schools. P2I has since gone on to develop a range of products and services all at the cutting edge of disability inclusion: 'Power House Games' involve the coming together of schools, corporates and civic groups to participate in teams together. P2I's first ever virtual Oxford-Cambridge boat race attracted rowers from both university crews, disabled counterparts scattered digitally across the country and raised thousands of pounds.

Southern Policy Centre[14]

Was launched at the University of Winchester hosted by Professor Joy Carter, the University's Vice Chancellor. They keynote speakers were Rt Hon Greg Clark MP, then Secretary of State for Universities and Lord Adonis, the former Transport Secretary, and local MP Steve Brine. They were joined by Vice Chancellors, Local Economic Partnership CEOS and business, civil society and faith leaders from across Wessex. SPC is the first and only think tank for the Central South and has gone on to publish significant reports focused on social care, educational poverty, skills gaps, the role of open data in improving public services and participatory budgeting. It's partners and collaborations include those with MHCLG, BBCTV the Leaders of the South East Councils Group, NHS, New Forest National Park, Surrey, Hampshire, Southampton and Portsmouth Councils and the Centre for Towns led by Lisa Nandy MP.

Commonwealth Initiative on Freedom of Religion and Belief
Approached by Baroness Berridge who at the time was Chair of the All-Party Parliamentary Group on Freedom of Religion and Belief. The APPG was struggling with administrative and organisational capacity due to miniscule funding and yet had the opportunity to make a strategic step change contribution to FORB debates. Addo Accounting[15] provided the accounting at first at the CIC's expense. Linked In Solutions provided events management capacity organising close to 20 parliamentary events including the one where Labour first committed to a Prime Ministerial Envoy for Religious Freedom.

At every stage the CIC provided strategic support to introduce business planning to the group. In turn this led to the invention by CIC volunteers of a concept for a *Commonwealth Initiative on Freedom of Religion and Belief*. In turn CIC volunteers worked with the University of Birmingham to design, develop and win funding for £1.6 million from the Templeton World Foundation to resource a team of some six staff to develop academic and practical initiatives internationally. In 2017 the International Young Leaders' Network seconded one of its leadership scholars to the Church of England's International Office to support the organisation of a major global conference at the UN jointly between the International Parliamentary Panel on Religious Freedom, the Konrad Adenauer Foundation and the German and UK Embassies to the UN.[16] The German Deputy Chancellor spoke and senior attendees include Cabinet Ministers from across the globe and Lord Alton, the Bishop of Leeds, and Rt Hon Stephen Timms MP from the UK. In 2018 during the Commonwealth Heads of Government meeting in London the Archbishop of Canterbury hosted the Initiative at Lambeth Palace.[17]

The Hotwalls Studios[18]
Soon after our launch we were approached by the Council's Director of Leisure. He was hoping to develop designs and a bid to convert some arches near the Cathedral that took the form of sea defences. The hope was to invent a series of hubs in which start-ups could be developed, brought together and market themselves to customers and funders. We agreed to help with business planning, to provide mentoring and

back office to the ventures and to be formally included in the bid when it went in to the Coastal Communities Fund at MHCLG. With changes in administration, and also in Officer roles this collaboration got much harder then much easier.

The logjam was unbroken by Council Cabinet Member, Lynda Symes, and local MP Penny Mordaunt MP. Cllr Symes involved the CIC back in the partnership and our volunteers began attending joint planning meetings again. When the Hotwalls finally opened the CIC's, contribution was recognised and one of our ventures in residence, the Company of Makers, moved in to our studio for the first three years. As they grew they were in due course able to expand across the region and take on additional facilities for their work providing 'maker' opportunities for former service personnel with mental health challenges. The Cathedral Innovation Centre continued to support the Company of Makers and ran a series of small events at the Hotwalls.

Cathedrals and the Future

Portsmouth Cathedral is one of the smallest and comparatively least resourced in the country. It is not in one of major Core 8 cities or London. The actual financial turnover of the Cathedral Innovation Centre is itself still tiny. Its significance is not in the scale of what it has done or set out to do with varying degrees of success.

The learning, the focused mobilising of support by the Cathedral as a civic anchor, a civic partner and an open collaborator especially where social, economic and environmental needs are pressing though poses fresh questions: what models have other Cathedrals already trail-blazed? How much more public value could large Cathedrals, shrines and Abbeys unlock in the future? How comfortable can they be with 'doing' the Gospel in this way as much as in the speaking of it? Could this be a recovery of ancient monastic habits of hospitality, gift relationships and service to place rather than anything more self-dramatizing?[19]

The Portsmouth experience then raises matters for research but also a model for a conscious gathering of time, space, skills and other resources to make concrete things happen. Ideas that have consequences bring mission to real life.

Might every Cathedral, Shrine or Abbey have the potential to drive an innovation or a web of innovations that will give people a chance to start real life again after crime or illness, life course disruption or even

Forum

Covid 19? It is a question which, seven years on, Canon Nick Ralph and I are still exploring. There is new work to be done on the applied 'science' of Cathedrals in this regard.

> *Francis Davis is Honorary CEO of the Cathedral Innovation Centre and Visiting Professorial Fellow in the Institute of Ageing Population at the University of Oxford.*

Notes

1. L. Francis (ed) (2015) *Anglican Cathedrals in National Life: The Science of Cathedral Studies*. Palgrave.
2. This is a focus of the work of the President of the English Benedictine Congregation's Working Group on the Future of Abbeys After Covid 2020 of which the present author has been a member.
3. See F. Davis et al (2008) *Moral But no Compass: Church, Government and the Future of Welfare* (Matthew James/Von Hugel).
4. Thousands of hours of another volunteer also, the late Alan Lihou, without whom none of the successes would have been landed.
5. I was myself at the front end of recovery from trauma caused by violent crime. Many of those we worked with were on their way back from 'life course disruptions'. See A. Zaidi (2008) *Life course disruptions and their impact on income and living conditions in EU member states,* http://eng.newwelfare.org/tag/life-course-disruptions/#.X-8qSkB2vIU
6. https://www.thersa.org/blog/2013/05/re-inventing-faith-spaces-businesses-and-atheists-welcome
7. Very Rev David Brindley, Dean of Portsmouth, until June 2018 played an important part in the CIC's early work.
8. https://www.bbc.co.uk/news/business-30513600
9. https://www.businessmag.co.uk/portsmouth-innovators-offered-mba-scholarships-at-portsmouth-business-school/
10. https://www.portsmouth.anglican.org/news/2013/05/08/cabinet-minister-launches-250k-faith-in-enterprise-awards/
11. https://www.lichfield-cathedral.org/news/news/post/31-people-inspired---a-success
12. https://www.southeastlep.com/app/uploads/Jobs_Innovation_Making_the_South_East_the_Capital_of_Social_Enterprise.pdf
13. https://www.power2inspire.org.uk/
14. http://southernpolicycentre.co.uk/

15. Addo Accounting, Linked In Solutions, International Young Leaders Network mentioned in these sections are all CIC 'ventures in residence'.
16. https://www.worldwatchmonitor.org/2015/09/religious-freedom-network-should-be-as-outspoken-and-organized-as-the-extremists/
17. https://www.birmingham.ac.uk/schools/ptr/departments/theologyandreligion/news/2018/ciforb-archbishop-forum.aspx
18. https://hotwallsstudios.co.uk/
19. Alpha claims 24 million people have attended its courses since 1977. 1.3 million attend in a normal year. This compares with 2 million for St Paul's and Canterbury Cathedrals per annum and 20 million per annum at the single Marian shrine of Vaillkani in India.

Book Reviews

Reading Romans Backwards: A Gospel in Search of Peace in the Midst of the Empire
Scot McKnight
SCM Press, 2019, 220 pp., pbk, £19.99

If you begin with chapters 12-16 of the letter to the Romans and find out to whom Paul is writing then it is easier to identify what he is attempting to do in the rest of the letter, so contends Scot McKnight. Rather than being a textbook of Paul's soteriological thinking, the letter comes to life as a pastoral missive designed to encourage a lived theology of reconciliation amongst siblings. Its further missiological purpose is to proclaim what peace truly is in the very heart of the empire.

In Romans 12-16 we meet the two factions, the Weak and the Strong. The Weak are predominantly Torah-observant Jewish Christians, perhaps returned from Claudian exile and therefore socially and economically insecure. Influenced by the traditions of zealotry, they are chary of paying taxes. Lived theology for them, as those electively privileged, necessitates obeying the law and so they look down on those who have a more libertarian attitude. Indeed, the Strong are mostly gentile Christians of higher social status who believe they are freed from the law's demands, and who in turn look down on the Weak's scruples. The main problem is the contrasting attitudes to food. Table fellowship is politicised.

Paul's 'fear was denominations' (16). The unity, solidarity and diversity of the Christian mission was imperilled by such behaviours. McKnight stresses that Paul is by no means trying to force everyone onto the same page. Observance and non-observance of the statutes of the law find their place within the fold. But what is missing is the Christlikeness that would reveal to the Roman Christians that they are siblings called to share the same table.

The rest of the letter is Paul's rhetorical means of getting them where he needs them to be. The aim is a Spirit-led Christoformity that would see them embrace one another and where power and privilege will be ceded for the sake of a radical peace, right where it matters. This will orient them to God, to life in the Body of Christ and orient them towards a public life where generosity and benevolence outstrip Roman civility.

So to fix the breach, Paul reassures the Weak that God is faithful – to the Abrahamic covenant. But faithful in ways that continually surprise (Romans 9-11): faithful in always raising up a remnant, faithful in sending Jesus as the Messiah, faithful in drawing the gentiles into the covenant as siblings. He then reminds the Strong that their God is faithful to his covenant with Israel. Jewish practice is not to be shamed. The Weak are their siblings within God's loving and expansive covenant. It is faith in Christ that is determinative for both groups, and is what will lead to a lived theology that reflects the faithfulness of God.

One of the most interesting parts of the book is the way we are called to imagine Phoebe reading the letter out and eye-balling each group and even a particular representative of the Weak (the Judge). McKnight's exegesis of Romans 1-4 is the most complex part of the book as he outlines Paul's rhetorical strategy and explains whom Phoebe is addressing and to what end. Essentially Paul works to unsettle various claims to advantage and privilege and doubles-down on his insistence that it is faith in the one who is faithful that leads to a transformative praxis.

In the middle of the letter Paul turns to the theological rationale of this embodied and lived theology (Romans 5-8). Here the 'grace of Life in the Spirit' (143) is what will set them free to be a Christoform family.

McKnight gives us an excellent gift: a readable book on Romans. Footnotes are few and the sources are simply listed at the back. He does not lose us in exegetical minutiae but paints a picture of a particular community with pressing needs, adding just the right amount of background material on house churches and Rome.

It raises some questions about how we deal with purple passages that crop up in the lectionary, which might have some more wily rhetorical purpose and might not be quite what they seem. Yet, what McKnight shows is that no Pauline theology is without pastoral intent and no pastoral situation is redeemable without a nuanced telling of God's story in Christ.

Book Reviews

At the end he gestures towards the needs of the contemporary church. It would be too easy for us to identify ourselves with one party or another, to point the finger at others and map them onto the divisions in Rome. To do so is to repeat the deployment of power and privilege that puts the focus on our lives and fears. The real goal is for us to be sufficiently Christoform that we can sit at table as siblings and manifest Christ's peace in a troubled world.

Matt Bullimore, Corpus Christi College, Cambridge

Faith, Hope and Love: Interfaith Engagement as Practical Theology
Ray Gaston
SCM Press, 2017, 160 pp., pbk, £19.99

This book is grounded in the experience of living alongside and learning from people of other religions in the diverse contexts of Leeds and West Midlands. The voice here is authentic, honest, reflective, and grounded as it mines for wisdom. There is a passion for how we might live with difference, and for receiving diversity as a gift from God. Gaston also offers his reader a clear and rigorous methodology of practical theology. The chapters also reflect the skill of a theological educator whose methods and processes have been tested out in teaching (at the Queen's Foundation for Ecumenical Theological Education in Birmingham). Conversation partners, and especially an impressive range of writers and ideas, are named with carefulness and skill.

Any institution struggling for coherence and survival might be excused for indulging in self-preoccupation. Whilst this may be the case for some churches in this country, Gaston asks us to look outwards and reflect on what kind of society we live in in the UK. There are many alternatives to Christianity. Debates over how we account for religious decline, particularly in relation to secularism, continue to shape public understanding of the nature of religious life and our comprehension of the many and complex practices that surround religion. We live in a society of many faiths and traditions. This should be seen as an opportunity rather than a threat in a country attempting to deal with systemic racism and its colonial past, and we should properly question whether Christianity can continue to have a privileged place in the public square.

Book Reviews

Gaston faces some of these theological questions. He deals with issues of truth in this pluralistic ecology where the binary claims of exclusiveness and inclusiveness are held, debated, and preached. Where are we to look for truth? Has a liberal theology that so shaped the interfaith movement from the 1970s run its course? What kind of theology will equip people of faith to live together and learn from each other? This book names many of the core questions with insight, but also the potential errors and conflicts that emerge from the violence that all religion has capacity to perpetrate and perpetuate.

The argument invites the reader to take multifaith consciousness seriously. It demonstrates the opportunities that are present in and through a careful attentiveness to the other. Gaston offers a very different model of theological exploration to enable being present is these situations of encounter. A dialogical theology that affirms the necessity of what Gaston calls an 'intra-Christian engagement' can enable witness, agency, and action. The reader is offered models for what is described as a more radical engagement which draws people together, listens to the variety and diversity of story, and builds community. We need from this perspective, the book shows, a different kind of contact and dialogue. Finally, the book invites the reader to prioritise engagement with Islam. Gaston states, 'the challenge of engagement with Islam for the Euro – American Christian is, I would maintain, an opportunity for growth and renewal in an age of spiritual and theological malaise in our Church.' (p.x).

Divided into two parts, the first part is an exploration of the method and practice of a practical theology of interfaith engagement grounded in the contexts within which Gaston has worked. Chapter 2 on the post-9/11 context is especially powerful in the way in which ethnography is used to deepen wisdom through engagement with praxis. Peace church traditions and the Wesleyan understandings of the way of salvation are used to explore how engagement might be a means of grace and an opportunity to deepen reconciliation.

Part two reflects on Islamophobia and multiculturalism in the complex context of competing political versions of truth in South Birmingham. These two chapters had resonance with this reviewer in the light of some of the contradictions and complexities of modern British life emerging out of these pandemic months. There is a comprehensive and helpful index, detailing the many primary and secondary sources that Gaston has drawn upon. They indicate a breadth and depth of learning which finds its shape in this illuminating

Book Reviews

and accomplished book.

My copy will find its way to Sarum College library, but most importantly some of the learning represented here will certainly find its place in the formation of students for authorised public ministry. Gaston has established himself as an innovative and original practical theologian and we should look forward to further work from his engagement and study. This is practical theology at its best.

James Woodward, Sarum College and the University of Winchester

Queer and Indecent: An Introduction to Marcella Althaus-Reid
Thia Cooper
SCM Press, 2021, 224 pp., pbk, £19.99

Thia Cooper's remarkable new book offers an introduction to the thought of Marcella Althaus-Reid, and revives the critical lens of indecent theology. Althaus-Reid's language is sometimes not easy to comprehend - probably because of the metaphors she uses from Latin American contexts, and also because her theology is too paradoxical to get an easy grip on her main points. Cooper's writing is therefore very useful in clearing up elements of confusion and general misunderstanding in Althaus-Reid's writings. Due to Cooper's personal experience of working with Althaus-Reid for her Masters and doctoral degrees, she is able to offer her first-hand observation of how Althaus-Reid thought and what she might mean in her writings.

The book has 13 short chapters, which introduce step-by-step different themes of Althaus-Reid. In Chapter 1, a brief biography sets out how Althaus-Reid, originally from Argentina, grew to have a connection with Europe and eventually settled and taught in Edinburgh, Scotland. Chapter 2 sets up Althaus-Reid's foundational critique of theology and the church for detaching themselves from real human experiences and so excluding social activism from theologising. Chapter 3 demonstrates how Althaus-Reid re-activated her hermeneutical circle from liberation theology in order to pay attention to the excluded (not only the poor). This leads to Chapter 4, which highlights Althaus-Reid's critiques of Latin American liberation theology and feminist theology. These critiques mainly focus on the idealisation of the poor and women, with real people being replaced with ideas. Althaus-Reid argued that the hermeneutic circle should not become closed: 'A systematic liberation should not exist', and '[t] here should never be *one* theology of liberation but a continuing spiral of action and reflection' (p.44).

Chapter 5 recognises how Althaus-Reid brought a post-colonial approach into her critique of Latin American liberation theology. Seeing that Christianity in Latin America was not yet decolonised enough to embrace the racial other, she welcomed the perspectives of indigenous people and the excluded to subvert the homogeneity of the prevalent theology. Chapter 6 explains that, for Althaus-Reid, the exclusion of marginalised people is further framed by capitalism. When Latin American liberation theology does not consider all the excluded, it has declared that liberation theology is ultimately still working with and replicating colonial theology from their oppressors. Althaus-Reid challenges us, 'Have we really seen those who even cannot be recognised by the system?': 'While some critiques of capitalism focus on exploitation, there are people so disconnected they cannot even achieve exploitation. The excluded do not participate in the market' (p.66).

In Chapter 7, Cooper helps us see the feminist side of Althaus-Reid—who explored the concept of God as a female prostitute. This controversial claim conjures a shocking image, but Cooper explains it in a simple way. 'The fact that we cannot see God in a sex worker shows us that we do not believe all to have the fact of God. Yet God and Jesus exists in each of us' (p.80-81). The image of God as a prostitute is a test for us and should help us see the connection between women's poverty and God. In addition, the consideration of women in Althaus-Reid is not the *idea* of women but their real bodies. By means of emphasising incarnation, in Chapter 8, Althaus-Reid reminds us that 'God did not rescue humanity from being human; instead, God became human through Jesus. This changes our relationship to bodily loving God' (p. 87).

All these critiques emerge into Althaus-Reid's famous proposal—indecent theology—as these oppressions all rely on the stability of the current structure of heterosexuality. Chapter 9 outlines Althaus-Reid's account of in/decency. *Indecenting* should be understood as a method of examining what we have been taught,; bringing our suspicions to bear on these teachings in theology, politics and sexuality; and being honest about our own experiences (p. 102). Maintaining our critical reflection on the relationship between reality, God and society is both constructive and deconstructive. Following Althaus-Reid's subversion

Book Reviews

of heterosexuality, Chapter 10 presents her bisexual approach to rejecting the dualism of the heterosexual system by means of thinking process over fixity. The trinity can be perceived in this concept of bisexual God.

This understanding of doing theology in process is what Althaus-Reid means by 'queering'. In Chapter 11, Cooper sums up by saying: 'If I speak about my experience, I acknowledge it as valid but not universal. To be queer and to queer is to do a theology that remains in process' (p. 126). This helps us clarify the distinctive nature of Althaus-Reid's queer theology—which is not just a theology of and for LGBT people but about our expansion of knowing God and accepting difference. Leading up to Chapter 12, Cooper explain why Althaus-Reid emphasised the marginality of God as God wants to go in exile because God cannot squeeze into a small box. And in Chapter 13, Cooper concludes the book by highlighting Althaus-Reid's understanding of crucifixions and resurrections (which in my view, has been underestimated by others). Althaus-Reid requires us to honestly recognise the horror of the death of Jesus—which is enacted daily by indigenous and other excluded people in our daily life. But 'death enables resurrection, to experience life anew' (p. 151). And this is the purpose of *indecenting* theologies.

Queer and Indecent successfully fills a lot of the gaps which may confuse readers of Althaus-Reid's writings. Cooper also sheds new light on reading them through engaging broader senses of queer theory, indigenous studies, postcolonialism etc. Beyond doubt, this *systematic* reading of Althaus-Reid is helpful, although it is far from certain whether Althaus-Reid herself would appreciate the *decenting* of indecent theology!

Yin-An Chen ,Westcott House, Cambridge

Book Reviews

Coming Home: A Theology of Housing
Eds. Malcolm Brown and Graham Tomlin
Church House Publishing, 2020, 192 pp., pbk, £14.99

Coming Home: A Theology of Housing is the latest in a series of theological offerings by the Church of England that seek to address pressing social issues of the day. The collection of essays is the fruit of the report of the Archbishops' Commission on Housing and includes essays from a variety of contributors with the aim of providing 'stimulation for those Christians working in the housing industry, professional theologians interested in this vital aspect of modern life, and Christians committed to building better communities in their neighbourhoods' (xvi). Its main achievement is to spell out clearly why, as Christians, we should be concerned about the affordability and availability of decent homes.

Graham Tomlin's opening chapter draws a narrative arc from Scripture reflecting the values highlighted in the Commission's report, that housing should be 'sustainable, secure, stable, sociable, and satisfying' (p. 14). His opening reflection that 'each one of us has a home' (p. 1) is perhaps unfortunate given the reality of homelessness, especially in light of its predicted rise as a result of the pandemic.

Tim Gorringe underlines the importance of sustainability, justice, community, empowerment, beauty, and life as theological priorities for housing. Stephen Backhouse offer a defence of neighbourhood as a primary Christian concept for any contribution to housing: 'what Christians bring to any national conversation about neighbours is the realisation that, when it comes to loving others as they truly are, neighbourhoods are bigger, more real, and a more important category to Jesus than nationhoods will ever be' (p. 51). Malcolm Brown highlights some of the ecclesiological assets afforded to those of us who are Anglicans in offering a theology of parish and place.

Sam Wells' essay stands out as a piece of reflection on the lived experience of living in an area of social "deprivation". He offers a robust theological exploration of the language of 'deprivation' and the limits of urban "regeneration", concluding that 'while urban regeneration seems to be a rival model of redemption, and thus an idol, it can prove to be a stimulus to the Church's reflection' (p. 89).

Shermara Fletcher, Angus Ritchie, and Selina Stone's chapter draws on Roman Catholicism and Pentecostalism to offer an important corrective to the Anglican tendency 'to view social issues

Book Reviews

such as housing from the perspective of the privileged and the powerful more than that of ordinary citizens' (p. 91). Their chapter offers a definition of community organising alongside well-chosen Catholic and Pentecostal examples of good practice which can help Anglicans combine 'discernment with a form of social engagement that emphasise the agency of the poorest' (p. 107).

Niamh Colbrook offers an account of creatureliness which she suggests must be borne in mind for any practical discernment as to what to the Church should advocate. She argues that our creatureliness requires 'communities of activity and agency in which they become themselves, and in the process afford the possibilities for other creatures to flourish' (p.121). She argues that the Church's practical discernment in this area must take account of our creatureliness and recognise that we are habit-making by nature. Moreover, the societal habits through which the housing crisis has emerged 'are malformations of the very processes through which we are made to flourish, and thus strike at our creaturely integrity' (p. 124).

Mike Long's chapter both challenges the stigma associated with social housing and contains a welcome survey of existing solutions to what he notes is 'not one single housing crisis but many, generated by a common dynamic but whose character has its own particularity' (p. 129). He argues that 'we need more social housing - but the key issue of all concerns the kind of communities we want to be: Diverse, plural, strong, participatory' (p. 143).

Florence O' Taylor asks whether 'through the lens of Christian friendship and mutuality, which sees the person clothed with dignity rather than diagnosis, might the Church offer a loving response that disrupts the current models of housing that leave the vulnerable with precarious housing or none at all, and instead promote participation in providing solutions' (p. 162). She highlights the lived experience of women whilst reflecting on the challenge of recent 'stay at home' orders for those who lack safe and secure housing. A final chapter by Nicola Harris and Jez Sweetland provides some practical examples in the form of three case studies of Christian action on the 'mandate to build communities of hope' (p. 184).

Coming Home contains a range of material to inspire Christians to play our part in building a consensus that action is needed to address the housing crisis. It stops shorts of spelling out clearly how Christians might be involved, whilst providing theological rationales for engaging with the work of the Archbishops' Commission. It is a helpful tool for Christian leaders and practitioners in engaging Christian communities to begin to act, in order to make good on the theological obligation articulated here to deliver decent earthly homes for all. Whether Coming Home inspires such action will be the crucial next step in its reception. Ensuring such homes are built and enjoyed by all will be a testament to the theology of housing articulated here, and a powerful means of witness to the heavenly home to which we are called.

Simon Cuff, St. Mellitus College, London

Confronting Religious Violence: A Counternarrative
Eds. Richard Burridge and Jonathan Sacks
SCM Press, 2018, 270 pp, hbk, £25

Arising out of perspectives on the history, development, present-day manifestations, and possible resolutions to the animosity between Judaism, Christianity and Islam, this collection of essays originated from a symposium in the 'Humble Approach Initiative' of the John Templeton Foundation. The 'Humble Approach' invites scholars from different disciplines to examine a contentious topic, with the aim of learning from one another's experiences and standpoints, and finding constructive ways forward. In practical terms, some chapter suffer from being presented on the two-dimensional page rather than in real life – where the more technical presentations could be elucidated by questions and discussion, or enhanced by images. The collection is book-ended by reflections from the late Rabbi Jonathan Sacks (whose previous publication on religious conflict, *Not in God's Name*, inspired the symposium), demonstrating his gift for expressing complex ideas in lucid prose.

The key questions under examination are: Is it right to blame religion for the conflict it is often accused of causing; or is conflict inextricably linked to human psychology, and something which religious practitioners, theologians and educators strive to overcome? And: Is religion inevitably a tool of extremists, nationalists and totalitarians; or does monotheism, in particular, foster universal love and peace?

Each article is expertly argued, drawing on a huge range of disciplines from scholars around the world: politics, history, sociology,

Book Reviews

anthropology, biology – to name but a few. A recurring theme is how, seen through the lens of different academic approaches, religion operates as a key marker of identity, and how that depth of feeling can too easily be ignored by even well-meaning secular players. (The fact that not all secular authorities are sympathetic to religion is perhaps an under-explored aspect of the picture.)

Eliza Griswold reflects on her journalistic and international development experience in Africa, witnessing how religion became a primary definition of identity and meaning when national boundaries were arbitrarily drawn by colonialists, and peoples were left unsupported by their governments. Her overview of African religious history shows how little we Northern Europeans know about it. Similarly, it would be fascinating to hear more about the lessons for both sides which can be drawn from the history of early Christian/Muslim relations mentioned by educationalist Amineh Hoti, in 'Empathy and Policy in the Age of Hatred'.

A particularly fascinating contribution by anthropologist Scott Atram traces the search for authority, certainty and significance in troubling times through totalitarianism, and – more recently – populism, with an eye-opening analysis from a real-life perspective and social scientific methodology, complete with graphs and charts mapping the overlaps and interactions of identity and ideology. This provides evidence of something obvious to believers, but not usually spelled out so objectively to policy-makers: the reality that to their followers, religious and spiritual beliefs are life-changing and concrete, and ignored at their peril by those who think they can simply rationalise fanatics out of their destructive convictions. ('Prevent' programme: take note.)

A similar theme is taken up in his philosophical analysis of the relationship between compassion and reason, by Marc Gopin. Philosophers, he suggests, have tried to be too logical in their attempts to reason away religious prejudice; but he ruefully admits that the ideal of all religions eventually finding within themselves resources of compassion and tolerance towards other world-views is perhaps overly rosy and romantic.

Another intriguing analysis of religious belief and behaviour, by David Sloan Wilson, presents a biological/evolutionary perspective. Not only seeing groups of people as life-forms ('superorganisms') in themselves, in relation to whose interests both altruism and violent behaviour can be understood, Sloan also goes so far as to analyse

Book Reviews

the usage of particular texts and themes by different churches as if they were genetic material. Recording the incidence of Biblical references and interpretations in preaching and teaching produces a 'cultural genome sequence' which accurately maps on to degrees of fundamentalism, conservatism, liberalism, or tolerance. Ideological diversity amongst religious groups can thus be generated from the same 'genetic' building-blocks, in a similar way as biological diversity develops amongst living organisms. (The resulting DNA-type bar-chart would have been much better in the original colours and a larger format.)

The book challenges both secular and religious influencers. If secular leaders need to take more seriously the strength of religious feelings, rather than treating them as adjuncts to politics or aberrations from reality, religions themselves need to take more seriously how their tenets can be used to fuel violence and antagonism. Toned-down interpretations of texts like Luke 14:26 ('Whoever ... does not hate ... even life itself, cannot be my disciple') or the near-miss sacrifice of Isaac, which are often presented as metaphorical or symbolic, hide in plain sight the extremities of action they represent.

Jonathan Sacks concludes with his trademark emphasis on hope; but this collection highlights the extent of work still to be done in confronting and countering religious violence, if we are to truly bring in God's just and gentle reign of peace.

Carol Wardman, Ceredigion, Wales

Connect! Contemporary crises and everyday faith

Susanna Gunner
The Diocese of Norwich, 2020. Six booklets each of 16 pages. Printed copies or downloadable pdf format from: www.dioceseofnorwich.org/connect

This series of booklets explores the relationship between Christian faith and some of the most pressing issues of our time. It presents in a compact and insightful way the very sort of issues with which Crucible constantly tries to engage. If the engagement of this journal could be described as more intellectual and less practical, then that is a good reason to recommend such an excellent set of practical short booklets.

Susanna Gunner is Diocesan Spirituality and Discipleship Adviser, and

Book Reviews

also a Chaplain to the Queen. She has long experience in education and the Church's work with children. But here she has turned her attention with skill and expertise to subjects for adult reflection and response.

Each of the six booklets has a one word title: **Home, Work, Waste, Food, Neighbour, Nature**. Each then unfolds the word and the subject, so that the ethical challenges come gently sliding into our laps. Thus '**Home**' leads us straight into housing and homelessness, digging deep in a brief space, but not hectoring nor trying to copy the typical charity letters and leaflets by which we are all sometimes bombarded. The same kind of concise unfolding takes place with each subject in turn.

Each booklet is both attractive and serious. There are headlines, photos, excellent artwork, light-touch biblical and spiritual resources, poems, prayers, local statistics, inspiring stories, agency links – and lists of useful websites.

Sometimes, as with '**Food**', the introduction is about joy and blessing, eg the power of shared food, before the ethical punch of the crisis comes along, in the form of the politics of food, hunger and drought. The dignity of '**Work**' moves to a concentration on modern slavery. When it comes to the final subject '**Nature**', it might seem too difficult to make a simple leap from gift to challenge. How can anyone, in a mere page or two, move from the beauty of creation to the emergency of a warming world? But as a discussion starter for any group with a Christian ethos, it is enough. (Television documentaries are not afraid to make such leaps, all within a few minutes).

Since the set was produced in the first place by and for the Diocese of Norwich, it is not surprising to find several examples or stories with a local reference to Norfolk. These give an authentic flavour, and do not diminish the universal importance of each of these crises and their demands on our faith.

This is an outstanding set of booklets for church leaders, group study or personal use. I was so struck by their excellent content and presentation that I must warmly recommend them to a wider readership. Some in my local team of churches picked them up for Lent, but 'any time of year is good'. And I want to ask: why can't churches produce more resources of this quality? If you were doubtful on seeing '16 pages' for each booklet at the top of this review, I can only say to you that, sometimes, *less* really is *more*.

Edward Cardale, Welwyn

Order *Living in Love & Faith* and the accompanying course book from Church House Publishing

01603 785925 | www.chpublishing.co.uk

CHEQUE OR CREDIT CARD	DIRECT DEBIT
Individual rate UK: ☐£22	☐£20
Institutional rate UK: ☐£40	☐£35
Individual international: ☐£40	
Institutional international: ☐£50	
Individual copy ☐£7	

Please complete section 1. Cheque **or** 2. Credit/Debit card **or** 3. Direct debit (the name and address you give must match the information on your credit/Debit card/bank statement.)

YOUR DETAILS (Please complete]

Title .... Christian name .... Surname ....

Address: ....

....

....

Postcode .... Daytime telephone no ....

Email: ....

- I enclose a cheque for the total amount of £..............
  payable to Hymns Ancient and Modern Ltd.
- To pay by credit/debit card please visit www.cruciblejournal.co.uk/subscribe or contact us on 01603 785911

Ancient & Modern

Instruction to your bank or building society to pay by Direct Debit

Please fill in the whole form using a ball point pen and send to: Hymns Ancient & Modern Ltd.

Name and full postal address of your bank or building society

To: The Manager   Bank/building society

Address

Postcode

Name(s) of account holder(s)

Bank/building society account number

Branch sort code

Service user number: 2 4 3 2 3 3

Reference

Instruction to your bank or building society
Please pay Hymns Ancient & Modern Ltd Direct Debits from the account detailed in this Instruction subject to the safeguards assured by the Direct Debit Guarantee. I understand that this instruction may remain with Hymns Ancient & Modern Ltd and, if so, details will be passed electronically to my bank/building society.

Hymns Ancient & Modern Ltd, 13a Hellesdon Park Road, Norwich NR6 5DR

Signature(s)

Banks and building societies may not accept Direct Debit Instructions for some types of account.

This Guarantee should be detached and retained by the payer.

The Direct Debit Guarantee

- This Guarantee is offered by all banks and building societies that accept instructions to pay Direct Debits
- If there are any changes to the amount, date or frequency of your Direct Debit Hymns Ancient & Modern Ltd will notify you 10 working days in advance of your account being debited or as otherwise agreed. If you request Hymns Ancient & Modern Ltd to collect payment, confirmation of the amount and date will be given to you at the time of the request
- If an error is made in the payment of your Direct Debit, by Hymns Ancient & Modern Ltd or your bank or building society, you are entitled to a full and immediate refund of the amount paid from your bank or building society
  - If you receive a refund you are not entitled to, you must pay it back when Hymns Ancient & Modern Ltd asks you to
- You can cancel a Direct Debit at any time by simply contacting your bank or building society. Written confirmation may be required. Please also notify us

www.ingramcontent.com/pod-product-compliance
Lightning Source LLC
Chambersburg PA
CBHW022021290426
44109CB00015B/1267